Roger & Judy -

hopefully this recalls
mostly good times -

Judith & Bill

1975

The Yale Scene: University Series, 1

·1701·

Reuben A. Holden

Yale: a pictorial history

New Haven and London
Yale University Press
1967

Designed by Alvin Eisenman and Sheila de Bretteville,
set in Linotype Garamond 3,
and printed in the United States of America by
The Carl Purington Rollins Printing-Office of the
Yale University Press.
Distributed in Canada by McGill University Press.

Library of Congress catalog card number: 67–13439

Published with the aid of funds
given in memory of George Parmly Day
and Norman Vaux Donaldson.

*To Alfred Whitney Griswold,
sixteenth president of Yale,
whose vision made Yale the greater*

Preface

In planning a new and revised version of *The Yale Scene,* all of whose photographs were taken by Samuel Chamberlain, I sought contributions from students, faculty, and the public, as well as pictures from the files of the University Archives, the *Yale Daily News,* the *Yale Banner,* Class Books, the *Yale Alumni Magazine,* and the University News Bureau. I am therefore indebted to many sources, credit for which (where known) is given in the appendix. Particular thanks go to Yale's long-time photographers, Charles T. Alburtus of the University News Bureau and A. Burton Street of the *Alumni Magazine,* and to John T. Hill, assistant professor of graphic design. Old pictures have been dated only when there was specific evidence; many photographs were, unfortunately, found undated. Contemporary photographs speak for themselves.

A detailed description of the University's buildings, past and present, can be found in the booklet, *Yale Buildings;* a full chronological listing, however, with donors and architects, appears in the appendix to this book.

I am especially grateful to Robert F. Sexton, for assisting in the assembly of the photographs and the textual matter, and to Lottie G. Bishop for her painstaking research. George D. Vaill, Sheila R. Hough, George E. Gillespie, and Philip A. Prince helped me in the early stages of preparation. Professor Alvin Eisenman inspired much of the content and directed the physical layout; Professor George Wilson Pierson, University Historian, was good enough to read and criticize the copy. But the book would never have been published without the two ladies whose special qualities of professional competence, patience, and good sense make such an effort as this a joy for any writer: Jane Isay, the editor, and Sheila de Bretteville, who did the graphic design. I might only have wished that a great Yale man and friend, Hollon ("Tute") Farr had been alive to add the contributions he would have made so effectively as Curator of Yale Memorabilia.

Reuben A. Holden

Cushing's Island, Maine
September 2, 1966

Contents   *All numbers refer to illustrations*

Preface

Introduction

Yale has represented different things to different people: a college for some, a university of graduate study for others, a laboratory and research center for still others. For all it is a tradition which since 1701 has stood for the pursuit of truth, for a strong liberal arts foundation in learning, and for training to serve one's fellowmen at home and abroad.

In 1892 a young Harvard philosopher, George Santayana, described Yale as perhaps only a Harvard man could: "Nothing could be more American that Yale. Here is sound, healthy principle but no overscrupulousness, love of life, trust in success . . . a democratic amiability. No wonder that all America loves Yale, where American traditions are vigorous, American instincts unchecked, and young men are trained and made eager for the keen struggles of American life."

Yale's strength has come from many sources: from its students, so many of whom have reached the pinnacles of their callings, from a devoted faculty, which has brought the University a skillful blend of teaching and scholarly talents, and from its graduates, whose interest and financial support are constantly re-enlisted in the cause.

This strength has been essential in carrying out, in President Brewster's words, the University's basic purpose: "to create an intellectual, artistic, and moral impact on the shape of worlds to come." The original charter of 1701, written in the days when only prospective clergymen and perhaps hopeful statesmen aspired to college, was more specific in its mandate in calling for "the training up of youthful citizens for publick employment in Church & Civil state."

Yale, with its strong collegiate tradition, emerged as a university more slowly than might have been expected. Ezra Stiles in 1777 had charted a "Plan for a University" before he became president, but it was left to President Timothy Dwight to carry out its first step by formally establishing the Medical Institution (1810), and by laying plans for the Theological Department (1822), and the Law School (1824). The celebrated Faculty Report of 1828 which defended the classical course against educational reform movements, became the Magna Carta of liberal education for colleges across the country. A Department of Philosophy and the Arts, from which sprang the Sheffield Scientific School, the Engineering School, and the Graduate School had its modest beginnings a generation later. The School of the Fine Arts was organized in 1865–66.

The name of Yale College was not changed by state charter to Yale University until 1887, and gradually it became more conscious of its wider role: Schools of Music and Forestry were added, and in due course the Schools of Nursing and Drama. Together with the great collections housed in the University's Library, Art Gallery, and Peabody Museum of Natural History, the graduate and professional schools contribute elements of discovery and research to the teaching of the College, just as the College brings strength to them. Yale is happily compact enough to foster a natural interaction between all these elements. Yale has also determined that these schools must be kept in the forefront of their fields. Excellence has been the only criterion. Nationally preeminent in the days of the Sheffield Scientific School, Yale science, in particular, is reinvigorating itself as dreams of long overdue facilities are becoming a reality. New and distinguished structures are filling Yale's academic needs each year. Yale's 136 buildings now cover 163 acres (not including athletic areas) and represent many styles of architecture.

Although Yale's first building (1717) was on a half-acre site on the edge of town, New Haven fast grew around the College and made expansion complicated. But this has also made for close rapport, and the relative smallness of New Haven has helped Yale to remain an institutional community. Despite occasional quarrels, "town" and "gown" live in mutual respect. New Haven appreciates the cultural opportunities which are brought to the city, and Yale is happy that New Haven in 1716 outbid the other towns of Connecticut in providing funds and land for the permanent removal of the College from its early home in Saybrook.

Yale can also be grateful to the Colony of Connecticut for the appropriation of £500 to pay for part of the construction of a "College house" in New Haven. After the Revolution, the State of Connecticut continued to give financial aid to the College, including funds from shipping and import duties, which made construction of the Old Brick Row possible. In return for this and subsequent assistance, the Yale Corporation included the six senior state senators (now replaced by elected alumni), the Governor, and the Lieutenant Governor of the State among its members.

In 1718 the first major private benefaction was made, a forerunner of some millions of dollars which have been contributed by graduates and friends. Elihu Yale, whose grandmother had married one of New Haven's founders, Theophilus Eaton, and who became a prosperous East India merchant and governor of Fort St. George in Madras, made a timely donation of nine bales of goods with £562/12s together with 417 books. The Trustees promptly christened the unfinished first building "Yale College," a name which soon became synonymous with the institution itself, until then known as "The Collegiate School." Yale's ten founding fathers were Congregational ministers; all but one were graduates of Harvard College, and the governing body until the beginning of the twentieth century continued to be dominated by clergymen.

Perhaps Yale's most significant building boom came in the early 1930s with the instigation of the "College Plan," providing housing and dining facilities for all upper-classmen (freshmen are affiliated with the college, but live on the Old Campus), together with faculty offices, a Master's house, and a library, as well as a social and extra-curricular program. From the first, Yale has considered the residential principle critical in the educational process, and now the twelve colleges also provide academic opportunities through seminar-type classes conducted by Faculty Fellows. So through this plan, shared pre-eminently by Oxford, Cambridge, and Harvard, Yale is able to provide the advantages of a small college amidst the intellectual opportunities of a great modern university.

Professor George Wilson Pierson, sums up the spirit of the Yale Campus: "Between the national leadership enjoyed by Yale's graduates and the strenuousness of its undergraduate life, the vigor of its social code, the distinction and earnestness of its faculty, and broad discipline of its course of instruction there has always been an intimate connection. And Yale still believes in character and fair play, in the learning and teaching of the truth. It remains, as it has always been, a nursery of scholars and a gateway to that life whose test is achievement and public service."

Yale: a pictorial history

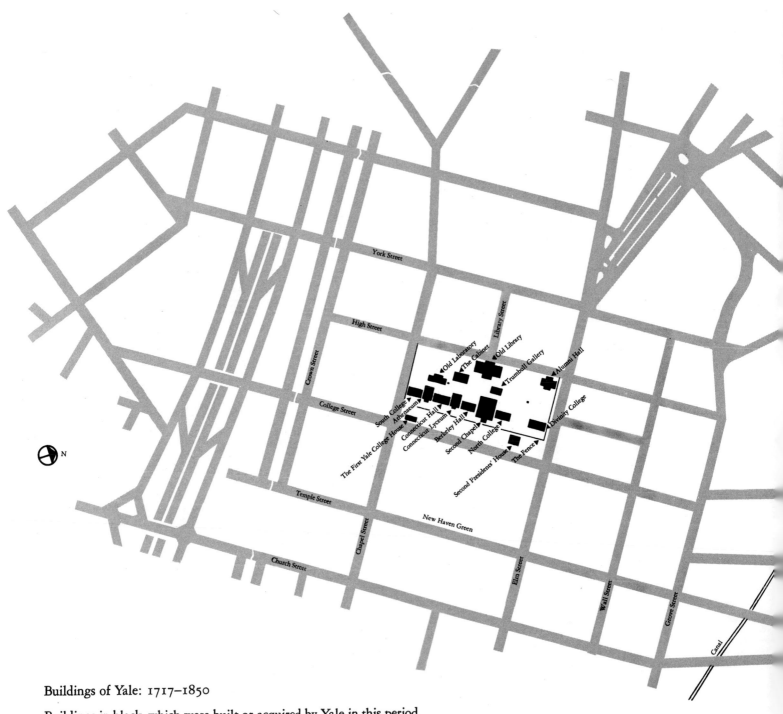

N

Old Laboratory ◄ ◄ The Cabinet ◄ Old Library

Trumbull Gallery ► ◄ Alumni Hall

South College ► Divinity College

Athenaeum ►

The First Yale College House ►

Connecticut Hall ►

Connecticut Lyceum ►

Berkeley Hall ►

Second Chapel ►

North College ►

Second Presidents' House ►

The Fence ►

York Street

High Street

Crown Street

College Street

Library Street

Temple Street

New Haven Green

Chapel Street

Church Street

Elm Street

Wall Street

Grove Street

Canal

Buildings of Yale: 1717–1850

Buildings in black, which were built or acquired by Yale in this period, appear in Part I.
Buildings in gray were built earlier but were still standing at this time.
The street grid is New Haven of 1966.

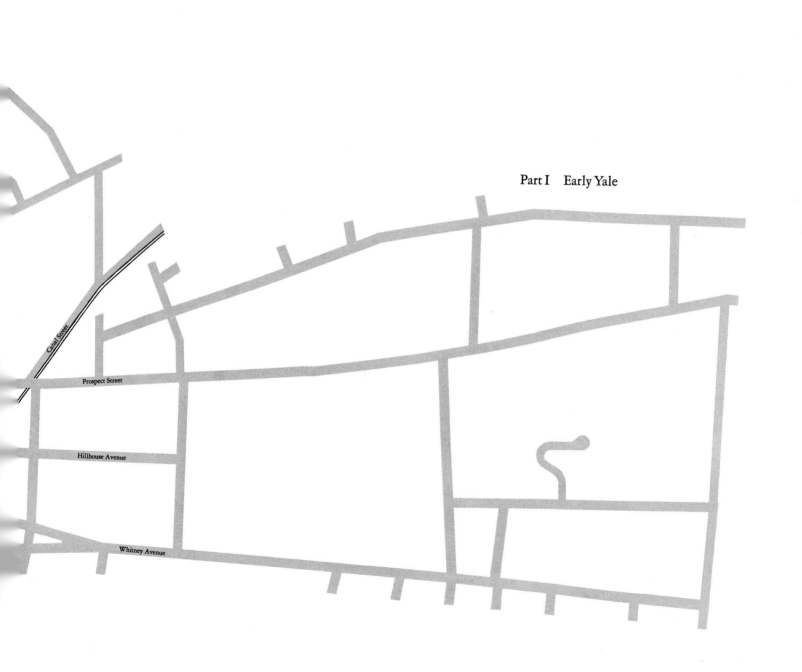

Part I   Early Yale

Canal Street

Prospect Street

Hillhouse Avenue

Whitney Avenue

1. The Samuel Russel House, artist unknown

The Samuel Russel House
(1700–1800)

In 1701, a group of ten Connecticut ministers met with the Reverend Samuel Russel in the south parlor of his Branford house to bring together plans for a college. The Reverend James Pierpont of New Haven and the Reverend Samuel Andrew of Milford were the leaders of the movement, along with Mr. Russel. According to legend, each man donated a number of folios, and as he placed them on the table said, "I give these books for the founding of a college in this colony." This informal act constituted for them the establishment of the school, and a request was then made for a charter. On October 9, 1701, the Collegiate School, whose purpose was to equip young men for service "in Church & Civil State," was formally founded by legislative act. The charter provided for ten trustees and a rector. At the first meeting in November they chose one of their members, the Reverend Abraham Pierson, as Rector and decided to locate the school in Saybrook. The doors to the original house now guard the entrance to the 1742 room in Sterling Memorial Library, whose collection contains at least nineteen books from the original donation. The books and doors are the only remaining souvenirs of this earliest building which saw the birth of Yale. Thus was Yale founded on an endowment of books. This initial contribution was followed shortly by similar gifts from Elihu Yale and Bishop Berkeley.

2. The doors to the Samuel Russel house, which now stand in the 1742 Room, Sterling Memorial Library

3. Inside the 1742 Room

The Saybrook Years (1701–1716)

The quiet Branford meeting and pledge of books set the style for the next 15 years of the school's life. The founders had chosen the unassuming name "Collegiate School" partly because they did not want to lead the Colonial authorities to suspect that they and the Connecticut Assembly were acting with too much independence; commencements were held in private until 1710 out of fear of attracting notice – and therefore interference – from London. The books donated in Branford became the least distinguished of the collection when the school received its first major donation in the form of nine crates of books bought and paid for in England and sent to Boston. In these crates was probably the finest library in Connecticut. It brought to the school and scholars some works that were unknown to the founders, among them Newton's *Principia,* and classics of English literature, and, oddly enough, an Armenian dictionary. The need for a place to house these books and the growing number of scholars was partially solved when the Assembly voted a grant of £500 for a permanent building. This sparked a battle over the choice of a place to settle the school. New Haven was finally chosen because more money was raised for the school from the residents and because the town made a donation of eight acres of land "at the end of the town" for the school. Thus began the centuries of Yale in New Haven.

By the Gov'r in Council & Representatives
of his Maj'ties Colony of Connecticot in Gen'll
Court Assembled, New-Haven, oct' 9: 1701.
An act for Liberty to erect a Collegiate School.
Whereas several well dispossed, and Publick Spirited Persons of their sincere Regard to &
Zeal for upholding & Propagating of the Christian Protestant Religion by a succession of Learn-
ed & Orthodox men have expressed by Petition their earnest desires that full Liberty and
Priviledge be granted unto Certain Undertakers for the founding, suitably endowing & Order-
ing a Collegiate School within his Maj'ties Colony of Connecticat wherin Youth may be in=
structed in the Arts & Sciences who thorough the blessing of Almighty God may be fitted

4. The Charter of the Collegiate School, granted by the Colony of Connecticut, October 9, 1701

5. Whitehall, Bishop Berkeley's home in Newport, Rhode Island, was given to the College by Berkeley

The Collegiate School chose to settle in New Haven in 1716

6. The *Chronicle* View of New Haven, published in the *New Haven Chronicle* from April 1786 to April 1787

and moved there in 1717.

October 1746

	Dyar	Tilch Palmer Mitchel	Reynolds Palmer	Coleman	Loomis December Blague	Smith	Cook	Newel Beard Dee Sperman Hart
Munson Sumner Bartlet Newel	Brown	Hall Lyman	Mills Clerk Crane		Huntington Maltbie	Cook Hubbard	Benedict	Fish Mead
Library	Strong	Mr Whiting Stam	Mr Fisk Brainard	Fitch	Mr Adams & Cotton november Burton Buel	Mr William Hall		Wolcott Pitkin Shelden
The Hall		St Russel Russel	Johnson Baldwin Bennet		Cuyler Stocking Elderkin Doggel	Porter William Smith		Ripley Lothrop Welch marston

7. President Clap's floor plan of "bespoken rooms" in the Yale College House, October 1746

The First Yale College House (1717/18–1782)

Disputes over the design of the first Yale College House are settled by this bas-relief on Bingham Hall, based on Norman Isham's definitive research. Built in 1717–18 and dedicated at the 1718 commencement, the building was named in gratitude for the recent gifts of Elihu Yale. It contained a kitchen, a combined dining room and chapel, a library, and "50 studies in convenient Chambers." The floor plan of "bespoken rooms" was drawn by President Clap.

8. A plaque on the wall of Bingham Hall, based on Norman Isham's reconstruction of the first Yale College House

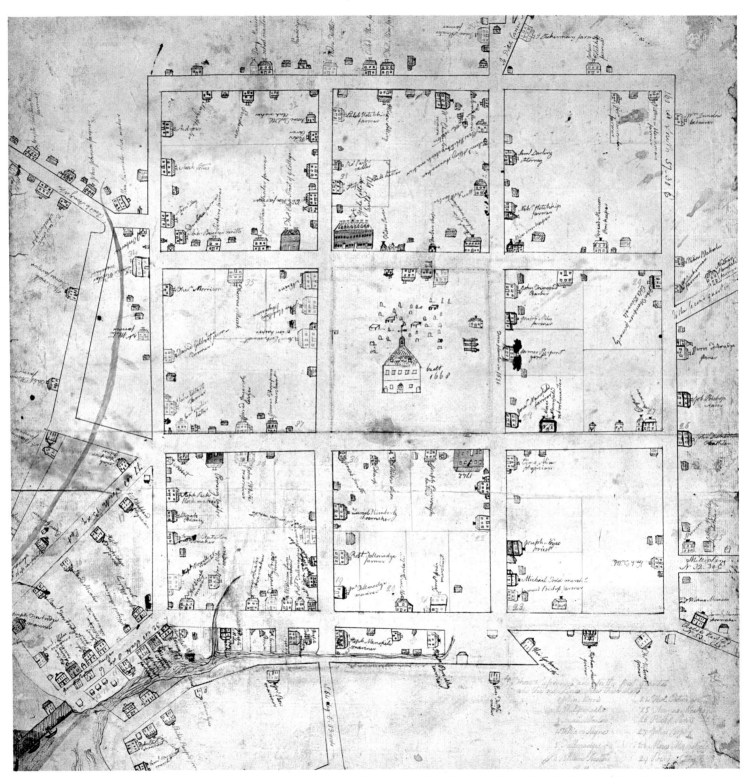

9. "Plan of the City of New Haven Taken in 1748," by James Wadsworth, Class of 1748. The Yale College House faces the Green, and President Clap's house is across the street

Sixty years of peace were interrupted with a Revolution,

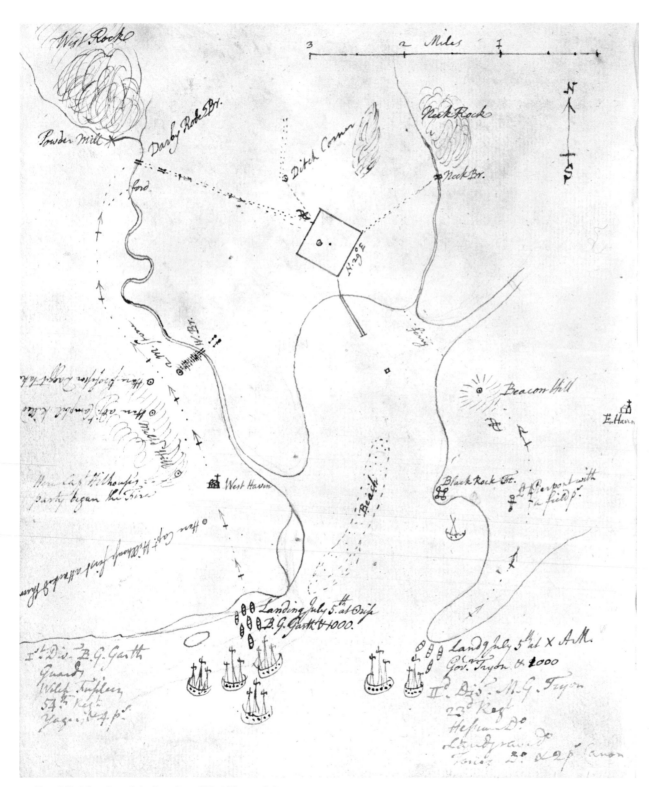

10. **Ezra Stiles' drawing of the invasion of New Haven, July** 1779

The Revolution

During the years of the Revolution,
conditions in New Haven became
difficult for students and tutors alike.
Food was scarce in March 1777, and
it was deemed wise to move to nearby
Connecticut towns. In the Welles
house, Glastonbury, sophomores and
juniors lived and had classes. Ezra
Stiles, President, discovered the
tactics of the British landing in July
1779, and recorded it in his journal.
George Welles, captain of the
Student Company in the July 5,
1779, invasion of New Haven by
the British, here protects the
Athenaeum and Connecticut Hall.
His courage and the prowess of the
Student Company may have saved the
day, but tradition has it that the
British considered the buildings too
handsome to burn.

11. The Welles house, Glastonbury

12. George Welles, Class of 1779, Captain of the Students' Company at the invasion of New Haven, defends the College buildings. From a watercolor by St. John Honeywood, 1782

but Yale with Ezra Stiles endured.

13. "A Front View of Yale-College, and the College Chapel, New-Haven," printed by Daniel Bowen from a woodcut, 1786.
   Students near President Stiles take off their hats, a time-honored custom

Yale after the Revolution

Ezra Stiles, the first Yale graduate to be regularly elected president, conceived a "plan for a university," the basic pattern for the organization of most American universities. Stiles "remained more interested in what he did not know than in what he did," says his biographer, Edmund Morgan. He was president during the final years of the Revolution and a financial depression, but the College emerged stronger than ever. Academic standards were raised, and student enrollment reached 270 – 100 more than at Harvard. It was during this period that an amendment to the charter was approved, providing that the Governor, Lieutenant Governor, and six senior State Senators sit as trustees on the Yale Corporation, in return for "substantial financial assistance." The First Chapel, to the left of Connecticut Hall, was erected with college funds. It was never heated, in accordance with contemporary fashion. A graduate of that time recalled "the grand and far-renowned President of Yale taking his place in the pulpit of that unwarmed Chapel, buttoned to the throat in a closely fitting, drab-colored, great-coat, with mittens on his hands, and so going through the devotional services." Students were traditionally rowdy – burning the college privy, rioting in Commons over bad food, mutilating library books, fighting with sailors from ships docked in the harbor – to the point that Stiles, in referring to his job, said: "The Diadem of a President is a crown of thorns."

Dec. 30. 1780

14. A pencil drawing of President Ezra Stiles, by St. John Honeywood, 1780

Connecticut Hall began the Old Brick Row.

15. John W. Sterling and roommate in Connecticut Hall, 1863

16. Interior of Connecticut Hall, gutted during the 1953 reconstruction

Connecticut Hall (South Middle College) (1750/53–)

Connecticut Hall (known as South Middle in the 19th century) is the earliest member and sole survivor of the Old Brick Row. It was named in honor of the Colony Assembly, which secured the building funds through an authorized lottery and the sale of a captured French frigate and its cargo. The "College built in a very Elegant and handsome Manner" was not completely finished until 1756. By the 1860s South Middle had become the most unpopular hall and its occupants were the poor and unlucky. A Yale historian of that period described it as "dilapidated, scabby and malodorous with the must of ages." One poor boy lived there, John W. Sterling, who walked from Stratford, carpet bag in hand, in 1860, and later left Yale an enormous bequest. When, years later, Connecticut Hall was threatened with demolition, memories of the unpleasant accommodations vanished in a flood of nostalgia, and a group of impassioned alumni united to save it. The building was renovated in 1882, restored to its original exterior in 1905, and gutted and completely redone in 1953, with the aid of a grant from the Old Dominion Foundation; in 1965 it was designated as a National Historic Landmark. During the second decade of the 20th century, the building caught fire, and Yale President Hadley, '76, U.S. President Taft, '78, and Major Archie Butt, stood by.

17. Hadley, Taft, Butt, and others watch a fire in Connecticut Hall, January 20, 1912

18. The fire in Connecticut Hall

19. A spring day in 1862

20. Athenaeum

Athenaeum (First Chapel) (1761/3–1893)

Freshmen may have regretted the generosity of the British in sparing the First Chapel, remodeled in 1824 as the Athenaeum for recitation and dormitory rooms. The original spire was replaced by an octagonal tower to house a telescope, and legend has it that Professor Elias Loomis encouraged students climbing up behind him to observe the heavens with: "Turn to the right, turn to the left, release the limb." The illustration shows the building in its final appearance after 1870, when a revolving cylindrical dome was mounted on the tower.

South College (1793/4–1893)

"South College, second entry, second floor, front corner" represented the best of all possible dormitory accommodations, and the building was almost entirely pre-empted by seniors. The second floor was preferred by privileged upperclassmen because it avoided both the damp and cold of the first floor and the long trek to the upper stories. There were thirty-two rooms, or "chambers," in each college; a "chamber" usually consisted of a main sitting room with fireplace, two bedrooms, a "clothes press," a washroom, and a coal closet. The popularity of South College was undoubtedly due to its focal place on the yard and its proximity to Chapel Street and the Fence. Senior pranks abounded at this time, and one harassed tutor described his stipend as "$500 a year, free room, and coal *thrown in.*"

21. South College

22. A student room in South College

with decorated rooms and decorous ceremonies.

23. The room of a Spoon Man in North Middle

Berkeley Hall (North Middle College) (1801–1895)

Built on part of the land purchased to displace the town jail, the poorhouse, several taverns, and other unsightly neighbors, North Middle was named Berkeley Hall to commemorate Bishop Berkeley's aid to the young college. The architecture of the Old Brick Row – once considered elegant – was, in the 1860s, felt to be disquietingly similar to the decaying factory buildings populating the East. This mattered little to the students, who were more than satisfied with the life of the Row, if not its beauty.

24. A rainy Class Day in 1896, on the site of North Middle College. This picture was taken from the Old Chapel

25. North Middle College

26. The Lyceum, built by Peter Banner

Connecticut Lyceum (1803/04–1901)

The first building to be designed exclusively for teaching and study, the Lyceum relieved the congestion in the dormitories, where classes were often held in the entryways. In the cellar, where space was designed for teaching the new discipline, chemistry, Benjamin Silliman's laboratory endured for fifteen years, despite rapidly rusting apparatus and chemicals spoiled by the underground moisture. Above the cellar, Lyceum became a location for pranks. A recitation would start on the third floor, when from a passageway very much like a tunnel came a tramp, tramp, tramp – and football men with cleated shoes walked in. The lecture had hardly resumed when footsteps and the bump of a baseball bat announced new arrivals; next it was tennis, each fellow with racquet in hand. Professor Northrop looked them over and with a happy smile said, "When will the crew be up with the boat?" "Major," retriever mascot of '96, became a regular member of French recitations; the instructor waived regulations and cited him as a pattern of behavior for the class. The Lyceum was also a target for snowballs, and the tower clock was constantly being defaced. It is said that only after the clock was removed could the college carpenter be spared to take the first vacation of his career. The bell in the tower was successively inverted and filled with freezing water, gagged, and ingeniously pealed at the oddest hours.

27. Gracious living in "Lyceum Flats"

and prayer.

28. Second Chapel

Second Chapel (1824–1896)

Here, for many years, morning prayers convened at six on winter mornings and at five o'clock during the summer. Students sat on hard benches (only faculty stalls were furnished with cushions, which had a way of being "abstracted" to feed celebratory bonfires), but there were a few corners where one could pray, lean, doze, or perhaps whittle – to which last activity the scarred benches bore silent witness. When Battell Chapel was ready for use, the building was rechristened "Old Chapel" and its steeple continued to inspire climbing feats.

North College (1820–1901)

When North College was new, its rooms were preempted by seniors. But by the 1880s there was little to distinguish it from other Row buildings: "Each had its sagging beams, its billowy floor, its cracked ceiling . . . and, as to other arrangements, sanitation shrieked."

29. Interior of the Chapel

30. North College, where students received their mail at Yale Station

The Old Brick Row was a face to meet the town,

31. A View of the Buildings of Yale College at New Haven, including the five southernmost buildings of the Old Brick Row in 1806 (South College, Athenaeum, South Middle College, Lyceum, and North Middle College), with students playing football on the Green, drawn and engraved by A. B. Doolittle

and from the Fence groups viewed the town.

32. The Fence, rounding Chapel and College Streets, in front of the Old Brick Row

33. Looking from Elm Street. North College and Old Chapel on the left, the Treasury **right**

The Fence

"Night and day it receives innumerable rivulets of common leisure . . . Thigh to thigh sit scholar, athlete and Bohemian, in a guild of fellowship far better than the dusty ruts of learning." As much an invitation to leap over as a barrier, the Fence defined where gown left off and town began. Its round, comfortable rails provided a convenient perching place and became the center of college life. The homely structure, carved thick with initials, found its way into the life of every undergraduate. There was, of course, a rigid seating plan: seniors and juniors occupied a generous stretch facing Chapel Street, and sophomores had a short piece facing the Green. Freshmen were rewarded with a small tailpiece if, and only if, they emerged victorious from their annual baseball game with Harvard; then they moved on to Chapel Street and "were enthroned proudly on the sophomore rails." When, in 1888, President Dwight proposed to move the Fence from the corner of College and Chapel streets to provide a site for Osborn Hall, a hue and cry arose from undergraduates and alumni alike. Vociferous protests on the part of 2,100 graduates from all over the world were in vain, however, and the Fence was transplanted to its new place within the quadrangle. There it made a fine perch for watching senior baseball, but some of the heart of a venerated tradition was gone.

34. Seniors on the Chapel Street side of the Fence

35. The Cabinet

36. The Old Laboratory, with the Art Building behind

The Cabinet (1819–1890)

This building drew its most durable name from the mineralogical collection housed in large glass cabinets on the second floor. Over the years, the Cabinet changed occupants and titles. It was dubbed the Philosophical Building when the departments of natural philosophy – physics and astronomy – made use of the facilities. Later it was called the Reading Room by students who enjoyed the opportunity to browse through the newspaper collection upstairs.

Old Laboratory (1782–1888)

The fourth building constructed at Yale, the old Laboratory contained the dining hall and kitchen, formerly in the original Yale College, and tales of students' constant skirmishing makes up part of its history. The story goes that students would fasten slices of meat or bread to the underside of tables as provisions against the possibility of the next meal's being scanty or unpalatable. In 1820, the building took on a new fame, as Benjamin Silliman's laboratory was moved here from the basement "Pit" in the Lyceum. The scene of several of Silliman's most celebrated experiments, the Laboratory was called "one of the most important centers of chemical science in America." This building also provided quarters for the Yale Co-op's first two years, from 1885 to 1887. The College Pump served as a watering spot and gathering place.

37. The pump beside the Old Laboratory

filled with galleries, laboratories –

38. Divinity College, at the end of the Row

39. The Second Presidents' House

40. Trumbull Gallery was transformed into the Treasury by the addition of windows in 1868

Divinity College (1835–1869)

The first home of the Divinity School, then the Theological Department, completed the line of buildings of the Old Brick Row. Close though it may have been to the hearts of the founders of Yale, it stood worlds apart from Yale College, whose students had little to do with the "theologues." Built with the proviso that the College might reclaim the property at a fair appraisal, Divinity College was razed in 1869 to make room for Durfee Hall.

Second Presidents' House (Analytical Laboratory) (1799–1860)

The residence of Presidents Dwight and Day, this building was turned over to the newly founded School of Applied Chemistry in 1847. The early School was an academic orphan, and its first two professors, John Pitkin Norton and Benjamin Silliman, Jr., bought their own apparatus and supported themselves on private student fees.

Trumbull Gallery (1832–1901)

This first college-connected art museum in the United States was built to house the collection of historical paintings by Colonel John Trumbull. The Gallery also housed the crypts of Trumbull and his wife, hence its tomb-like appearance. In 1869, windows were added, and it became the Treasury Building, for the use of the central administrative offices. The paintings and crypts were moved to what is now Street Hall and later to the Art Gallery.

41. The buildings between the pumps: Trumbull Gallery, the Cabinet, and the Old Laboratory

42. The Old Library

43. Inside the Linonia and Brothers in Unity reading room on the second floor

Old Library (1842)

A contemporary commentator called this Early Victorian Gothic building housing the University Library the first college building to make any "pretensions to architectural beauty." Its pre-Raphaelite style struck a new note in campus architecture, and its cost "fell short of thirty thousand dollars." At the time it was begun, the library catalogue listed 10,000 books. The Linonian Society and Brothers in Unity, religious societies, collected their libraries of light fiction in order to attract membership. Their competition meant larger and larger libraries, which were housed after 1842 in two wings of the Old Library. The separate staffs of the collections were united with the central library administration in 1871, but the books have remained separate in catalogue and housing. The building became known as the Old Library in 1889, when a much-needed annex, Chittenden Hall, was completed. Additional library space was created with the construction of Linsly Hall in 1906/07, between the Old Library and Chittenden, and all books were finally removed to the new Sterling Memorial Library in 1931. At that time, the Old Library was remodeled and became Dwight Memorial Chapel (it was originally built to resemble a Gothic chapel) and the Yale Christian Association (Dwight Hall), which serves as a focal point for student religious and social service activity.

44. The main reading room of the Old Library, which became Dwight Memorial Chapel

and Alumni Hall, primarily for exams.

45. Loyal unionists pull down the secession flag from the tower of Alumni Hall, 1861

Alumni Hall (1850–1900)

Alumni Hall was the site of tribulation and jubilation, as here students took admissions tests and came twice a year thereafter to write their examinations. Celebrations after the exam period were held every other year at the Biennial Jubilee, where skits, dinner, and Biennial hats enlivened the occasion. In due course it became a yearly event. But more of a good thing became too much, and Annual hats were never in as great demand as the Biennial. Yale students' loyalty to the northern cause brought excitement during the College's Civil War years; here loyal unionists tear down a secession flag from a tower of Alumni Hall. These towers now stand at the entrance of Weir Hall.

46. Examination room, Alumni Hall

47. Biennial Hat

48. Alumni Hall

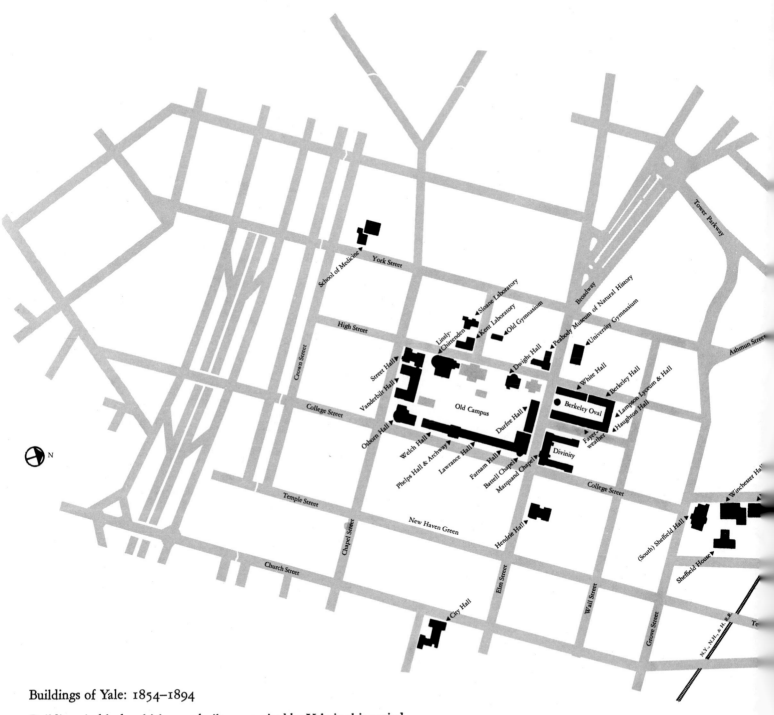

Buildings of Yale: 1854–1894

Buildings in black, which were built or acquired by Yale in this period,
appear in Part II.
Buildings in gray were built earlier but were still standing at this time.
The street grid is New Haven of 1966.

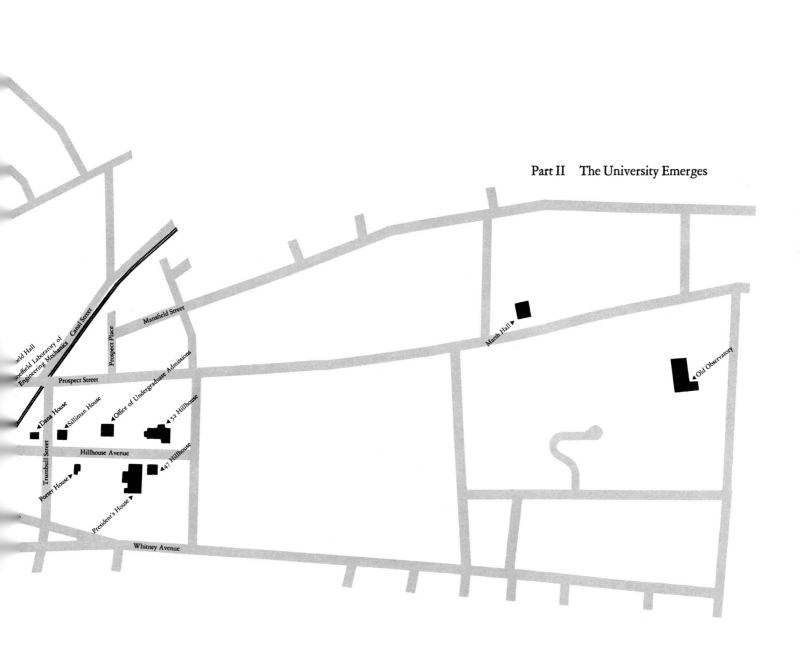

Part II   The University Emerges

Marsh Hall ▸

◂ Old Observatory

◂ Dana House

◂ Silliman House

◂ Office of Undergraduate Admissions

◂ 52 Hillhouse

Mansfield Street

Prospect Place

Prospect Street

◂ Mansfield Hall

◂ Mansfield Laboratory of Engineering Mechanics

Canal Street

Hillhouse Avenue

Trumbull Street

Porter House ▸

◂ 447 Hillhouse

President's House ▸

Whitney Avenue

At the heart of undergraduate life was the Old Campus.

49. Recent graduates, in costume, join older alumni on the Old Campus for a reunion in 1907

The Old Campus

Between 1717 and 1857, Yale College acquired, parcel by parcel, the entire block known today as the Old Campus. Benjamin Franklin had owned one piece of the land on which he intended to establish a printing-office. Part of his plot later held the town jail and almshouse. In the 1840s, when the need arose for more dormitory space than the Brick Row could provide, Yale began to erect its buildings at the street line to form a single, enclosed courtyard, an effective barrier separating the traditionally abrasive elements of town from those of the college. By the 1860s and '70s, the new building program was in full swing. The alumni now took on the financial responsibility the state had abdicated, and the Corporation replaced its six senior senators with six alumni. The new buildings enabled the college to carry on its daily life more privately; such mysterious ceremonies as Tap Day could be conducted in seclusion. The Trumbull Gallery and the Philosophical Building gave promise of a second line of structures to lie parallel to the Brick Row, but this plan was not carried out. Once the sacred preserve of the lordly seniors, The Old Campus has since the 1930s been the home of the Freshman Class. It is used fall and spring for informal sports. In June new grass is sown and a huge canopied platform erected for commencement exercises attended by over 10,000 graduates and guests.

50. The Old Campus after all but Connecticut Hall had been removed

51. The Old Campus when many of the original buildings were still standing

First came the choice of a place to live:

52. A view of Farnam Hall from the Old Campus. Battell Chapel to the left

53. The study of a suite in Farnam Hall, fourth floor

Farnam Hall (1869/70)

The opportunity to begin construction of a quadrangle to rim the sides of the college square was provided by funds given for a new dormitory or "college," as such buildings were then called. President Porter commented on the project: "This arrangement renders it possible to erect a succession of new buildings, as they shall be needed, without displacing a single one of the old. It also provides for the gradual abandonment and removal of the present buildings of the Brick Row, which, however uncomfortable and unsightly, are dear and venerable by many associations. Should the time ever come when the contemplated quadrangle shall be completed, no university or college now existing will be able to show a larger or more beautiful inner court, with two nobler rows of elms, than Yale College will then present." Farnam Hall was erected on the College Street site of the Second Presidents' House. The building can be entered only from the Campus, but this limitation did not result in a completely cloistered group of students. The windows on the street side were still available for enthusiastic shouts of "Fire!" when the bell-ringing fire trucks racketed through the streets. The heated controversy over the placement of the new college – alumni thought that the beauty of the square would be destroyed – generated suggestions that the college be removed to the outskirts of town. This pastoral vision of a center of learning beyond the city's clamor was often revived.

54. A view down College Street

55. Participants in the Pass of Thermopylae, in front of Durfee Hall

56. A view of Durfee Hall from the Old Campus, Battell Chapel to the right

Durfee Hall (1871)

At its completion, Durfee Hall
was the largest and most imposing
building on the Old Campus. Yale
then had 755 students, a faculty of 64,
and an endowment of $1,500,000.
It was fashionable to live off campus
when Durfee was put up; the older
buildings were obsolete and uncomfortable. At the turn of the century,
however, Dean Wright persuaded
several sophomores to "pack" two
Durfee entries with outstanding and
popular classmates, and campus living gradually became more desir-
able. Durfee's fame was enlarged by
a satire, *Dirty Durfee,* by Brian
Hooker, '02:
There's a place on the Campus, I
weel ken its name,
And the brawest o' views may be had
frae the same –
Gin there's onything doing ye're
wishful to see,
Why, it's up wi' the windows o'
dirty Durfee!
There's a braw time on Tap-Day,
when down by the fence,
A' the Juniors gang buggy, and sweat
most immense –
When ilka Keys heeler has jumps
like a flea,
Then it's up wi' the windows o'
dirty Durfee!
At the Pass of Thermopylae on the
night of Omega Lambda Chi, the
entire College, in costume, paraded
to celebrate the abolition of freshmen fraternities. After the parade,
freshmen ran the gauntlet of upper-
classmen.

57. Students arrive at the Elm Street entrance to Durfee Hall. The fire escapes have yet to be put up

as did Lawrance.

58. The Spoon won by Mr. Southworth, Class of 1863

Lawrance Hall (1885/86)

This freshman dormitory was built in memory of Thomas Lawrance, '84, whose position as chairman of the junior prom committee would have entitled him to be called the "Spoon Man." This honor, first bestowed to the junior lowest in academic rank, eventually became a colossal popularity contest. Presentation of the spoon at the junior promenade was the highlight of the Yale social calendar. As intellectual values replaced popularity, the furor over the spoon subsided, but it is still presented annually to the chairman of the prom committee.

59. The Spoon Committee of 1866

60. A view of Lawrance Hall from the Old Campus

Welch and Phelps provided needed space,

61. Roller skating in the court between Welch and Osborn. Connecticut is in the background

Welch Hall (1891)

A newer freshman dormitory, Welch was built in 1891 in English Collegiate style to relieve the High Victorian architecture of Farnam and Lawrance.

Phelps Hall and Archway (1896)

Phelps is the first building most freshmen and visitors see. Modeled after an English gatehouse, it completes the enclosure of the great courtyard, the Old Campus. It houses the University police, information offices, and the classics department.

62. A horse-drawn water wagon waits in front of Welch Hall on the then unpaved road around the inside of the Old Campus

63. Phelps Hall from the Old Campus. Through the gateway, the New Haven Green

and Vanderbilt was the earliest Gold Coast.

64. Looking across Chapel Street to Vanderbilt Hall

Vanderbilt Hall (1894)

When Vanderbilt Hall, the "Gold Coast," was built, the seniors took it over. There they played their brand of "old two cat" (baseball) with two bases, a tennis ball, and an old cane for a bat. The area was perfect for pranks: its outward courtyard, facing south, is a natural bridge to Chapel Street and a barrier between students and the eyes of faculty and campus police. Now a freshman dormitory, it still boasts the specially designed suite over the archway, a memorial to William H. Vanderbilt who died in 1892, a year before his graduation.

65. Maude Adams, Ethel Barrymore, and friends decorate this Vanderbilt room

66. Baseball in Vanderbilt court

The first women at Yale attended the School of Fine Arts.

67. Women students join in a still-life class in 1906

Street Hall (1854/66)

Although the first Art Gallery had been built at Yale in 1832, no art instruction had then been proposed in the faculty. The first School of the Fine Arts to be a part of a college was made possible by the munificence of a graduate, Augustus R. Street, '12, who resided in New Haven. In November 1864, the cornerstone was laid. The resulting structure became known as the Art School Building until 1928, when it was renamed to commemorate the donor. Besides studios and classrooms, the new building provided exhibition space for the paintings moved from the Trumbull Gallery and for the unique Jarves collection of early Italian paintings; space was also available for the display of sculpture. An Art Council was formed to plan this new educational program, and the school opened in 1869, the first Yale school to admit women. Classes were given in drawing, painting, sculpture, and art history. Architecture was added to the curriculum in 1908, and, more recently, city planning and graphic design. The degree of Bachelor of Fine Arts was first conferred in 1891, the Master's in 1927. In 1911 a wing was added without substantial change in the exterior appearance of the hall, and fifty years later the interior was completely renovated. With the building of new facilities for the School in 1963–64, Street Hall became the home of the department of the history of art and the Audio Visual Center.

68. School of The Fine Arts, shortly after construction

69. The main stairway of Street Hall, with plaster casts from which students drew

70. The chancel of Battell Chapel in 1882

71. Inside the Chapel during services

Battell Chapel (1874/76)

Daily attendance at services in this third of Yale's chapels was mandatory until 1926, and, as a result, student decorum was unconventional. There was a superstition to the effect that if the seniors, bowing reverently as President Dwight passed out of Chapel, were lucky enough to touch the hump on his back, they would have good luck in the day's recitations. The belief was strong, and preferred aisle seats often commanded a good price on the collegiate market. Other students chose to read newspapers. Competition for aisle seats, irregular behavior, and hasty entrances notwithstanding, daily chapel served many purposes, not the least of which were to gather the whole college together each day and and get all the students out of bed. Today Battell Chapel is the scene of the Sunday services of the inter-denominational Church of Christ in Yale University. They are conducted by the Pastor of the Church, who is also the University Chaplain. He delivers sermons twice a month, and his associates and visiting ministers preach on the intervening Sundays. The Chapel's architecture is "High Victorian Gothic." Its chimes ring at each quarter hour and serve as a constant reminder to the Freshmen living on the Old Campus that classes must be attended. Battell also houses memorials to members of the faculty and student body. The new apse was dedicated in 1947 to the undergraduate deacons who died in World War II.

72. Leaving Sunday Chapel

but not pool games in Dwight Hall.

73. Undergraduates shooting pool in the old Dwight Hall

Dwight Hall (1885–1926)

Next to Alumni Hall was this head-quarters of the Yale Christian Association, the scene of significant developments in the religious life of the University. In addition to meeting rooms for study groups, a variety of recreation facilities was provided. The building was removed to allow an unobstructed view of Harkness Tower, and the Association eventually moved to the Old Library. The organization gradually took on the name of its original building, "Dwight Hall," and assumed a wide extra-curricular interest.

74. The view from the first Dwight Hall, showing Welch, Connecticut, and Vanderbilt Halls and the Old Library in the background

75. Dwight Hall, covered with ivy, and the manicured shrubbery of the Old Campus

First books, then students, filled the new library annexes.

Linsly-Chittenden Hall (1888/90; 1906/07)

These two contiguous buildings, built almost twenty years apart, were renovated in 1930 after the completion of the Sterling Memorial Library. They had been wings of the old University Library, just to their north on the Old Campus. The elegant Tiffany windows in the Reading Room of Chittenden were a distinguished ornament to the building. Before more book stacks were needed and Linsly was added between them, Chittenden and the main library unit were connected by an eerie tunnel-like passageway. The remodeled facilities are used chiefly by the social science departments, including psychological experimental laboratories. The large lecture room on the first floor of Linsly is the scene of frequent lectures by visiting dignitaries as well as regular showings of special movies by the Yale Film Society.

76. The first landing of the main stairway, Linsly Hall

77. Chittenden Library before Linsly was built, c. 1891

78. Linsly Hall as it looked in 1908, with Chittenden to the left

79. Seniors exercise their privilege of spinning tops in front of Osborn Hall

Osborn Hall (1888–1926)

"Osborn, that fantastic dream in stone perched like a squatting toad with open lip."

The first important gift in the administration of Timothy Dwight the younger, Osborn completed the line of buildings designed to close off the Old Campus from the distractions of the growing town. Student interest was to be drawn inward, rather than outward. However, Osborn became the focus of widespread disapproval – from alumni who were bitter because its construction necessitated the removal of the cherished Yale Fence and from students who mocked its strange design. Students had difficulty concentrating on even brilliant lectures because of the deafening noise on cobblestones of horses and trolley cars rounding the corner. Here the famous lecture on the Battle of Waterloo was given annally after his retirement by Professor Arthur M. Wheeler, familiarly dubbed "Waterloo" Wheeler. Ex-President William Howard Taft, '78, who had come to New Haven from the White House to be Kent Professor of Law was one of those who suffered at the lectern. The steps of Osborn became a favorite place for playing tops, a popular game involving more prowess and exertion than the present-day sportsman might suspect. When, in 1926, Osborn was to be torn down, the seniors held a "keening." A solemn procession formed in Harkness and wound its wailing way across the Old Campus and through the old lecture halls where they had sat and learned.

80. Osborn Hall, at the corner of College and Chapel Streets

as Yale was becoming a University.

YALE UNIVERSITY
A General View of Existing Conditions

81. In his *Plan for a University,* John Russell Pope wrote, "Whenever possible, the arrangement as in the Old Campus should be followed." This is his rendition of the University as it was in 1919

The Berkeley Oval helped house the growing enrollment.

Berkeley Oval

The Berkeley Oval consisted of White Hall and Berkeley Hall (1893/4), Lampson Hall (1903), Haughton Hall (1909), and Fayerweather Hall (1900/02). In the center foreground stood the Round House, which provided space for the University telephone exchange. Yale Station inhabited the basement of Fayerweather with the *Yale Daily News* and the Bursar's Office. Though an ugly red in color and hardly prepossessing in appearance, the buildings of the Berkeley Oval contained the offices of some of Yale's most inspiring teachers. William Lyon Phelps had an office in Lampson, and "Johnny" Berdan's office was in the basement of White. The Oval, first the home of seniors, formed a rather dignified courtyard. In the 1920s, however, with the institution of the common Freshman Year, the new arrivals were housed together in this quadrangle. The tone of the area changed immediately. The tightly packed and highly volatile freshmen needed nothing more than a cry of "All out, Freshmen!" to set off a howling explosion of young men into the street. Riots like those that began in Berkeley Oval continued to be a way of life for freshmen during the raccoon coat and Stutz-Bearcat days until the early thirties, when the buildings were removed and other activities absorbed the unspent student energy. The two lions once installed in front of Lampson now guard the University Power House on Tower Parkway.

82. The '96 Board of the *Yale Literary Magazine* meets in White Hall

83. In and out of Yale Station, when it was in Fayerweather. The wagon sells roasted peanuts

84. Berkeley Oval. The circular telephone exchange stands in front of White Hall, Berkeley Hall, Lampson Hall, and Fayerweather Hall

85. (South) Sheffield Hall served the "Medical Institution" before 1858

86. In the tower of South Sheffield lived the "attic philosophers"

(South) Sheffield Hall (1860–1931)

The hotel built by College Treasurer James Hillhouse was never used for the entertainment of guests. Yale College purchased it for the "Medical Institution," which occupied it until 1860. The building acquired a sinister reputation because of its occupants' profession: a tunnel was rumored to lead across the street to the Grove Street Cemetery, and some townspeople believed that this enabled medical students to practice body-snatching. Joseph E. Sheffield purchased the building in 1859 and presented it to the Scientific School; he added two large wings, provided laboratory apparatus, and endowed a fund to support three professorships. In 1865 the building was again enlarged with the addition of a three-story structure connecting the wings and two towers; the front tower contained a belfry-clock and was surmounted by a revolving turret containing an equatorial telescope. The transfer of the early Yale Scientific School, as it was first known, from its cramped quarters in the Old Campus to adequate accommodations gave the Sheffield Scientific School identity as a separate institution, governed by its own Board of Trustees. The attraction of a faculty of distinction as well as the demand for engineers and scientists in the expanding economy resulted in an enrollment that increased steadily and a reputation for the School that was second to none.

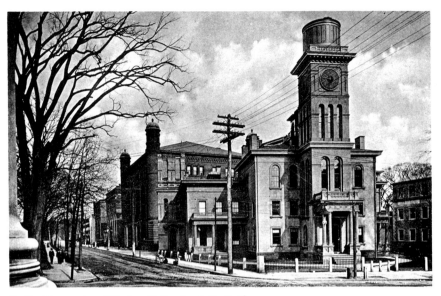

87. Looking out from Woolsey Hall to South Sheffield

88. An inner room

89. Beakers and funnels amid the pots and pans in the attic philosophers' kitchen

and medical research, and Divinity moved across Elm Street.

90. Students take the air on ledges and stoop of the old Medical School on York Street

91. Dr. William Hill Bean and anatomical model inside the old Medical School

School of Medicine (1859/60–1952)

This is the School of Medicine after its move to York Street from Sheffield Hall in 1860. In 1889 the City Dispensary was established next door to provide facilities for practical application of theoretical training. The School remained here until the Sterling Hall of Medicine was completed in 1924, when the building was used by the University of Connecticut College of Pharmacy. Here, in 1913, an agreement between the University and the General Hospital Society of Connecticut was arranged, providing the first formal affiliation between the School and the New Haven Hospital. Beginning in 1916, qualified undergraduates could combine their last two years of college with their first two at Medical School.

East Divinity (1869/70–1931)
West Divinity (1873/74–1931)

A prime reason for the existence of a college in colonial days was to offer candidates for the ministry a curriculum that would provide them with a breadth of learning. Nowhere else could they receive special preparation in ancient languages and theology. The Livingston Professorship of Divinity, the first chair at Yale, was established in 1746, although the position was not filled until 1755; and a department of theology was established in 1822. Because the dormitories in this building were frequently undersubscribed, poor freshmen often rented unused rooms on the top floors for as little as 50 cents a week.

92. Looking down Elm Street to the old Divinity School: Taylor Hall, Trowbridge Library, Marquand Chapel, and Edwards Hall

Law studies began, appropriately, in City Hall,

93. Law classes were first held here in City Hall, in the annex on the left

Hendrie Hall (1894/1900)

The Law School was first housed in the City Hall Annex on Church Street, following its founding by three prominent Yale graduates who conducted a private law school and had arranged a modest affiliation with Yale in 1824. The course of law, like that of art and science, was unsteady: recognition and encouragement from the College were not always readily won. Hendrie Hall was built in two stages and served the Law School from 1895 until 1931, when the Sterling Law Buildings were completed.

94. Inside the Law Library, Hendrie Hall

95. The Elm Street view of Hendrie Hall, the first Yale law building, now the hub of extracurricular activity

and the first Peabody Museum gave sanctuary to newly discovered bones.

96. The original Peabody Museum, as it stood on the corner of Elm and High Streets

Peabody Museum of Natural History (1873/76–1917)

Built on the corner of Elm and High Streets, the early Peabody Museum was given by George Peabody of London following the appointment of his nephew, Othniel C. Marsh, as the first professor of paleontology at Yale. A collection of fossil footprints from the Connecticut valley was installed in the basement; the Mineralogical Collection was moved from the Cabinet to the first floor; the second story was devoted to geology, and the third to zoology, each under the supervision of a curator. The open spiral metal staircase in this fireproof building helped to make required visits by school children exciting adventures. Professor Marsh achieved international fame by excavating hundreds of vertebrate fossil remains in a series of expeditions in the West, during which he braved hostile Indians and rival collectors. The collection aroused the interest of Darwin and Huxley, and the latter made a special trip to New Haven to examine it. Huxley was so impressed with Marsh's evidence about the evolution of the horse that he gave up his old opinions. Huxley wrote Marsh that his facts "demonstrated the evolution of the the horse beyond question, and for the first time indicated the direct line of descent of an existing animal." Meticulous attention to the preparation and assembling of fossil specimens was given by Fred Darby and Hugh Gibb, technicians shown here at work.

97. Kennedy and Reed with dinosaur bones, which went to the Peabody Museum

98. Hugh Gibb and Fred Darby hard at work preparing bone specimens in 1911

Engineers and astronomers did their research on Prospect Street,

99. **The Old Observatory**

100. Up Prospect Street, across from the Grove Street Cemetery, Winchester, North Sheffield, and Sheffield Laboratory of Engineering Mechanics

Old Observatory

These Prospect Hill buildings served the astronomy department until 1956, when city lights and smoke forced a move to Bethany.

Winchester Hall (1892)

Winchester's classrooms and laboratories have been used for courses in mechanical, electrical, and civil engineering. Today Winchester contains laboratories for research in the mechanics of solids and classrooms for general use.

North Sheffield Hall (1872/73)

North Sheffield was built at a time of financial stress for the Sheffield Scientific School. In 1870–71, total expenditures were $27,975, moving dangerously close to the entire income of the school. Only two years after the completion of this five-story classroom and laboratory building planned by a committee of professors chosen by Joseph Sheffield, there were complaints that insufficient space continued to make it necessary to turn away qualified students. Mr. Sheffield's wish to provide for the future of the school was evident in his will: his fortune was divided into seven parts, and the school shared equally with his six children.

Sheffield Laboratory of Engineering Mechanics (1894/95)

This building was erected as a chemistry laboratory. Following the completion of the Sterling Chemistry Laboratory, it was renovated for use by the School of Engineering.

101. Professor William A. Norton, in top hat, supervises engineering students in a simple field exercise in surveying in front of the Grove Street Cemetery wall

while Yale College scientists labored in Kent and Sloane.

102. Kent Chemical Laboratory, before the additional story was added

Kent Laboratory (1887/88–1931)
Sloane Laboratory (1882/83–1931)

Although these two laboratories marked an advance for the science facilities of the College (limited previously to the Old Laboratory and recitation rooms), they duplicated the Sheffield buildings. Sloane was used as a College physics laboratory until 1912, and Kent was part of the chemistry department until 1922. Perhaps Yale's greatest scientist (obscure though he was during his lifetime), Josiah Willard Gibbs, '58, worked in Kent when evolving basic theories of thermodynamics.

103. Chemistry studies advance as students experiment in Kent Laboratory in 1889

104. Sloane Physical Laboratory stood on Library Street until it was torn down in 1931. Gibbs' office was on the second floor, right of the tower

105. A ball game in 1897

Old Gymnasium (1859–1892)

Although a small outdoor gym was placed near the present Wright Hall as early as 1826, the Old Gymnasium on Library Street was Yale's first gymnasium building and the first to be erected outside the Old Campus. It marked a new direction in the "exercise of physical strength among the students." The era of impromptu brawls in town ended with the introduction of organized sports. It was perhaps no accident that the gym was located near the site of the old Fire Company Number Two, which had always attracted student activity (including the fatal shooting of a fireman in 1858). After the University Gymnasium was built in 1892, the Old Gymnasium became University Commons. Before the days of heavy traffic, the crew rowed regularly in the New Haven harbor. Boathouses here were used from 1859 until 1934, when rowing had to be moved to the Housatonic River at Derby.

106. The first public appearance of the crouching start, May 12, 1888. The 100-yard dash was won by Charles H. Sherrill, Class of 1889. On the left, Harvard loser

107. Crew champions of 1873

108. The early Boat House near Tomlinson's Bridge

109. The Yale Boat House off Chapel Street

110. The Old Gymnasium on the corner of Library and High Streets

reached a plateau in the 1880s and '90s.

111. Tug-of-war in front of Sloane Physical Laboratory

112. The University Gymnasium, on the site of the Trumbull College dining hall, was the first
Yale gym to have a swimming pool

University Gymnasium
(1892–1932)

The University Gymnasium, which
stood on Elm Street on the present
site of the Trumbull College Dining
Hall, crowned the glory of over two
decades of phenomenal Yale athletic
successes. Walter Camp would advise his protégés: "When you lose a
match against a man in your own
class, shake hands with him; do not
excuse your defeat; do not forget it;
AND DO NOT LET IT HAPPEN
AGAIN." Erected with funds given
by alumni, this building contained
a main exercise hall, lockers, baths,
a swimming pool, a Turkish bath,
two rowing tanks large enough for
eight-oar crews, two bowling alleys,
and a baseball practice room. In
the gym program emphasis was
placed on remedial training to correct
physical defects; thorough physical
examinations, given annually to
each student, indicated that the
average student's health improved
during his college years. In 1909 the
Carnegie Swimming Pool was erected
behind the gymnasium, and Yale
began its unbroken series of victories
in swimming meets. The first squash
courts, given in 1910, were built
in the gymnasium; additional courts
and bowling alleys were erected
nearby in 1915. The popularity of
squash was responsible for the subsequent construction of courts in
the residential colleges and in the
Payne Whitney Gymnasium.

113. Body building in the gymnasium. The indoor track was on the mezzanine

Marsh Hall (1878)

From 1878 to 1899 Marsh Hall was the home of Yale's great paleontologist, Othniel C. Marsh.

The Silliman House (1807)

The first house on Hillhouse Avenue, built by James Hillhouse, has been a University residence since 1926.

Office of Undergraduate Admissions (1892)

This Hillhouse Avenue home was acquired by the University in 1948.

114. Marsh Hall on Prospect Street, the original home of the Forestry School

115. The Silliman House before it was moved around the corner to Trumbull Street. The boat to the left is on the Farmington Canal, now a railroad cut

116. The Office of Undergraduate Admissions stands proudly on Hillhouse Avenue

117. The first home of the Drama School, 52 Hillhouse Avenue

118. Dana House, 24 Hillhouse Avenue

52 Hillhouse Avenue (1849)

Built for Professor John Pitkin Norton by Henry Austin, this house was purchased by the University in 1923 and now houses the Economic Growth Center.

Dana House (1849)

This Italianate villa on the corner of Hillhouse Avenue and Trumbull Street was designed by Henry Austin for Professor James Dwight Dana, whose fame as a geologist is recognized by the fact that his house has been designated as a National Historic Landmark.

Sheffield Mansion (c.1832–1957)

Sheffield Mansion was designed by Ithiel Town, one of the founders of the National Academy of Design and the architect of Center and Trinity Churches on the New Haven Green. Joseph Sheffield bought it in about 1859, and it was altered extensively by Henry Austin, as this picture, taken in 1874, shows. Originally Mr. Town's residence, it housed his large library of art and architectural books and displayed his art collection. The Sheffield Scientific School acquired the mansion after Mrs. Sheffield's death in 1889. It was then converted into laboratory facilities and used for biology, physiological chemistry, applied physiology, and electrical engineering. It was torn down and replaced by the new wing of Dunham Laboratory in 1957/58.

119. President Porter's house at 31 Hillhouse Avenue as it looked in 1892

120. President Angell's house on Hillhouse Avenue, c. 1924

121. The Sheffield residence on Hillhouse Avenue, designed by Ithiel Town, was used for laboratories after 1889

122. The original President's House before reconstruction.

123. The President's House as it looks now

The President's House (1871)

The last three presidents of Yale have lived in this home at 43 Hillhouse Avenue. It was built for Henry Farnam by Russell Sturgis, Jr., and bequeathed to the University for the president's house, subject to the life use of Mrs. Farnam and their youngest son. The original Victorian mansion was remodeled in 1934, and since then has taken on a Georgian splendor.

Hillhouse Avenue

Called by Charles Dickens "the most beautiful street in America," Hillhouse Avenue was laid out in 1792 as a private road by James Hillhouse to extend through part of his farm. Elm trees, planted on both sides of a wide avenue, grew to form a canopy over the wide street that lead to Sachem's Wood, the mansion built by Hillhouse's son in 1828. Residences of distinguished architectural design were erected between 1809 and 1870 for members of the New Haven community. Some of these houses are now occupied by officers of the University; others have been converted into departmental office facilities; still others have been torn down and replaced by laboratory buildings. The avenue was privately owned until 1862, when it was incorporated into the city. The Dutch Elm disease that has attacked the "City of Elms" caused the avenue to lose some of its early splendor.

124. Hillhouse Avenue with Sachem's Wood, the Hillhouse mansion, at the end of the street

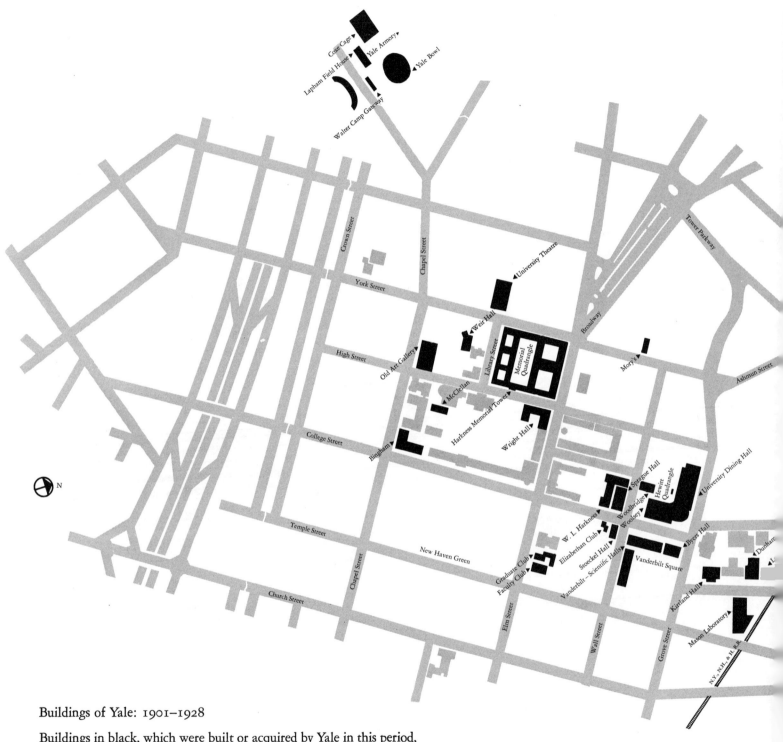

Buildings of Yale: 1901–1928

Buildings in black, which were built or acquired by Yale in this period,
appear in Part III.
Buildings in gray were built earlier but were still standing at this time.
The street grid is New Haven of 1966.

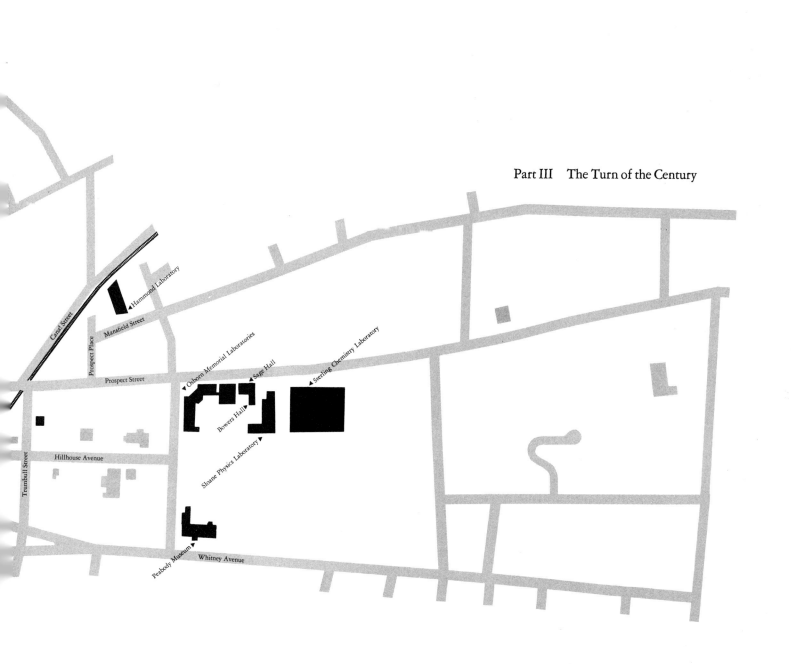

Part III   The Turn of the Century

Canal Street

Hammond Laboratory

Mansfield Street

Prospect Place

Prospect Street

Osborn Memorial Laboratories

Sage Hall

Sterling Chemistry Laboratory

Bowers Hall

Sloane Physics Laboratory

Hillhouse Avenue

Trumbull Street

Peabody Museum

Whitney Avenue

125. The University Dining Hall, decorated with College and School banners on Alumni Day

126. Graduates of the Class of 1906 join in celebration with older alumni

Bicentennial Buildings (1901/02)

The Bicentennial Buildings, erected with gifts from alumni to commemorate the 200th anniversary of the founding of the College, consist of Woolsey Hall, the University Dining Hall, Memorial Hall, and Woodbridge Hall close by. Although the heart of the College was to remain on the Old Campus, its "head" was now two blocks away at the corner of Grove and College streets, linking Yale College to the Sheffield Scientific School. Woolsey Hall, named for the tenth President of Yale, is an impressive auditorium seating 2,700. It provides space for major concerts, lectures, and special assemblies. Shortly after completion of the building, the Newberry Memorial Organ was installed. It has twice been renovated and enlarged by further gifts from the Newberry family. It is said to be one of the notable organs of the world, in both size and quality of tone. The University Dining Hall was designed to provide a Commons for all undergraduates, and it met this need more or less satisfactorily until the establishment of the residential colleges, each of which has its own dining facilities for residents, fellows, and visitors. One half of the refectory has since served the Freshmen as a dining hall. The remaining space is a cafeteria for other members of the University. Portraits of eminent Yale men decorate the walls; on special occasions a festive atmosphere is created by hanging University and College banners from the walls. The columns and cenotaph were added in

(continued)

127. World War I student formation in front of Commons, before the colonnade was erected

128. The Alumni War Memorial, dedicated in 1927

129. Aerial view of Woolsey Hall and domed Memorial Hall

130. The Hewitt Quadrangle at the Brewster Inauguration

131. Inside Woolsey Hall, President Brewster gives Baccalaureate Address in 1966

1927 as a memorial to Yale students who fought in World War I. The names of the battles in which they fought are inscribed above the columns. Memorial Hall, a circular building which connects the Dining Hall with Woolsey, has in its corridors tablets commemorating Yale men who died serving the country. On the second floor is the newly redecorated Presidents' Room, which is used for official University receptions.

Woodbridge Hall (1901)

Woodbridge Hall, given by the Misses Stokes of New York City to commemorate the Bicentennial, contains some of the University central administrative offices and the Corporation Room, on whose walls hang portraits of Yale presidents and the first patron, Elihu Yale. The building was named in honor of Timothy Woodbridge, a founder of the College. His name and the names of the other nine founders are also carved on the outside of the building. President Hadley was the first President to have his offices here. In the Corporation Room, each Fellow has a chair marked with his name on a brass tablet. When he retires, the chair goes to his home as the gift of one of his colleagues.

132. The President and Fellows meet in the Corporation Room, Woodbridge Hall

133. Carvings commemorate Yale's founding

134. Chestnut vendor in front of Woodbridge Hall before Ledyard flagpole was erected. Hewitt Quadrangle was then a grass court and later paved with cobblestone. A new granite pavement was laid in 1964

135. Byers Hall, today part of Silliman College

Byers Hall (1903)

Constructed to harmonize with the Bicentennial Buildings across the street, and modeled after the Petit Trianon at Versailles, Byers Hall was originally a social and religious center for the use of the students of the Sheffield Scientific School; its role was similar to that of Dwight Hall in Yale College. In 1940 the entrance stairs were removed, and the interior was remodeled to provide for the lounge, library, and fellows' suites of Silliman College, and for quarters for visiting scholars.

Vanderbilt-Scientific Halls (1903/06)

Until the erection of Van-Sheff, the Sheffield Scientific School had no dormitories of its own, although at the beginning of the century the school had an enrollment of over 800. The spirit of Sheffield, a source of wonder to Yale College students, was in large part due to the residential fraternity system. The Yale College students organized fraternities and societies by class; although they ate together, they were lodged in many different places. In contrast, Sheff's fraternities kept their members together for over two years and had residence halls adjacent to the "tombs." The courtyard of Van-Sheff was the scene of much of the school's extracurricular life. Now the Wall Street wing serves as a dormitory for Silliman, while the College Street section houses Law School students and the offices of the *Yale Alumni Magazine* and "Yale Reports," the University's weekly radio program.

136. Vanderbilt-Scientific Halls ("Van-Sheff") from Wall Street

137. The College Street wing of Van-Sheff

138. Byers Hall as it looked in 1902

scientific research was on the upsurge.

139. A 1914 geology trip on the train that runs on the Old Canal Line

140. Kirtland Hall, where geology was studied more formally

Kirtland Hall (1902/04)

This first laboratory to be built at Yale in the 20th century was named in honor of Jared Potter Kirtland, a member of the second graduating class of the Medical School. In the next twenty years, laboratory facilities were to increase sevenfold. The geology department occupied the building from 1904 to 1964, when it was assigned to industrial administration.

Sage Hall (1924)

This headquarters for the School of Forestry has facilities for research and teaching in forest entomology and wood anatomy. Bowers Hall was added in 1931 to provide an auditorium and soil laboratories.

Leet Oliver Memorial Hall (1908)

Leet Oliver was completed at a time when the popularity of the Sheffield "Select Course" made extra classroom space necessary. This three-year course of study that combined some of Sheffield's sciences with a liberal arts curriculum required no Latin for admission. It was a radical program for its time, offering courses in English, French, German, history, economics, and the early social sciences. Perhaps more liberal than the traditional Yale education, this Select Course offered students an opportunity for what was known, in future years, as "well-rounded education." After World War I, a year for all freshmen was added, and Sheffield became more closely related to the College.

141. A side view of Sage and Bowers Halls

143. Sage Hall, School of Forestry

142. Leet Oliver Memorial Hall

This meant a rapid increase

144. Dunham Laboratory

Dunham Laboratory (1912)

Dunham Laboratory looked like this before the addition was constructed in 1958. It is devoted to work in electrical engineering and houses the Engineering and Applied Science Library.

Sloane Physics Laboratory (1912)

In 1910 Mrs. Russell Sage, a descendant of Rector Pierson, donated funds for the Hillhouse property privately secured a few years earlier by Secretary Anson Phelps Stokes and other graduates who anticipated a land shortage. This space, called Pierson-Sage Square, was set aside to foster a new trend in the University; it would house a science center serving the several schools in common. Soon the faculty of each discipline would be reorganized into a University department. Physics was the first study to benefit, when Henry T. Sloane, one of the donors to Yale College of the earlier Sloane Physical Laboratory, offered to pay for a modern building. Erected on Pierson-Sage Square in 1912, Sloane Physics Laboratory provided facilities for undergraduate and graduate teaching and research. While admitting that the new building furnished an opportunity for much more adequate instruction than ever before, the Board of Trustees of the Sheffield Scientific School viewed with apprehension any procedure that would tend to reduce its control of departments originating in that school. Over thirty years were to elapse before the Yale Corporation completed this important consolidation.

145. Sloane Physics Laboratory

146. Osborn Memorial Laboratories, from the courtyard

Osborn Memorial Laboratories (1913/14)

The Osborn Laboratories consist of two wings, one originally designed for botany, the other for zoology.

Mason Laboratory (1911)

Mason was built for the study of mechanical engineering systems, thermodynamics, fluid mechanics, heat transfer, and combustion.

Hammond Laboratory (1904)

Hammond contains a lecture hall, museum, and laboratories for the study of metallurgy.

147. Osborn Laboratories, on the corner of Prospect and Sachem Streets

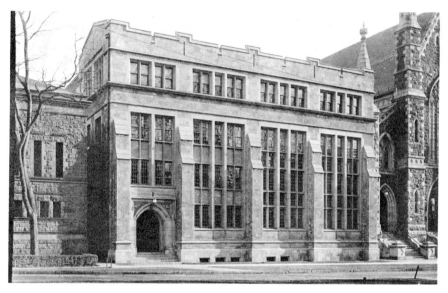

148. Mason Laboratory

149. Hammond Laboratory

150. Mason Laboratory before the major renovation in 1966

151. Hammond in the early days

152. Sterling Chemistry and Sloane Physics, with Sachem's Wood behind

153. Professor Gooch lectures to a Chemistry A 1 class

Sterling Chemistry Laboratory (1922/23)

The first building to bear the name of one of the University's most generous donors, Sterling Chemistry Laboratory was the third structure of the projected science center on Pierson-Sage Square. Following reorganization of the course of study and the receipt of new funds, chemistry was to consolidate in one outstanding laboratory for teaching and research. In the last quarter of the 19th century, Kent Chemical (for "Ac" students) and Sheffield Chemical laboratories were hailed as splendid additions to the teaching facilities. Professor Gooch is seen lecturing in a laboratory of Kent in 1915. Sterling Chemistry, following the tradition of academic halls in its appearance, cleverly concealed utilitarian demands with a saw-tooth factory construction roof over the central laboratory section. The industrial chemistry laboratory is two stories high. A large lecture room, research laboratories, faculty offices, a library, and shop and storage units are included. At the southwest corner of the building the statue of Benjamin Silliman, who introduced the study of science in the curriculum largely restricted to Greek, Latin, and mathematics, gazes benevolently upon succeeding generations of students. For twenty years after the completion of Sterling Chemistry Laboratory, the driveway leading to Sachem's Wood was forbidden territory, effectively separating chemistry and physics.

154. Sterling Chemistry Laboratory in the 1930s

The Memorial Quadrangle marked 200 years of Yale in New Haven.

155. Branford Court and Harkness Tower at the time of building

156. Dwight and Edwards entries, September 20, 1919

157. Workmen setting the first of eight finials of Harkness Tower, 4:15 P.M., April 8, 1921

158. Memorial Gateway from High Street

Memorial Quadrangle
Harkness Tower (1921)

The cornerstone of the Memorial
Quadrangle was laid on October 8,
1917. Construction, interrupted by
World War I and its aftermath, was
not completed until 1921. The academic procession for the inauguration
of James Rowland Angell on
June 21, 1921, was formed in
Branford Court. It was the wish of
the donor, Mrs. Stephen V. Harkness,
that the Harkness Memorial Tower
should honor her elder son, Charles
William Harkness, who had died in
1916. When her younger son,
Edward S. Harkness, furnished funds
ten years later to institute the
residential colleges, he met the
expense of converting the Quadrangle
into Branford and Saybrook Colleges.
Facing the problem of providing
"rooms for six hundred and thirty,"
architect James Gamble Rogers
wanted to avoid the usual dormitory
style and decided on a design similar
to the pattern lines of British collegiate quadrangles: a group of adjoin-
ing courts. The three large courts of
this quadrangle are named for the
towns associated with the early history of the University: Branford, Saybrook, and Killingworth. Wrexham
Tower, on the York Street side, was
modeled after the tower of St. Giles's
Church in Wrexham, Wales. Elihu
Yale worshiped there and his tomb is
in St. Giles's churchyard.
One of the world's finest carillons
was installed in the tower in
1966, and concerts are given by
the Guild of Yale University
Bellringers.

159. Harkness Memorial Tower above the roofs

160. Albert Arnold Sprague Memorial Hall

Albert Arnold Sprague Memorial Hall (1917)

Sprague Hall was completed in 1917, the first building erected exclusively for the School of Music. It occupies the site of the house of President Timothy Dwight the Younger. The old mansion was used by the Music School from 1900 to 1916. Besides an auditorium seating 728 and a stage accommodating 80 musicians, there are classrooms, practice rooms, a recording studio, and phonograph listening rooms for the use of students and faculty. In 1955 the first floor was redesigned for the John Herrick Jackson Music Library. Although the teaching of music at Yale began in 1854, not until forty years later did the department rank as a separate school with authority to recommend candidates for degrees. It is now a graduate school and awards the degree of Master of Music.

Stoeckel Hall (1897)

When the University celebrated the centennial of its first instruction program in music in 1954, it renovated the former Sheffield fraternity building, York Hall, and doubled the facilities of the School of Music, which had formerly been limited to the space in Sprague Hall just across the street. Stoeckel, Yale's only Venetian Gothic structure, was named in honor of Gustave J. Stoeckel, who had come from Germany to be the first teacher of music at Yale. The school's offices and studios were moved here, leaving enough room in Sprague to house a greatly expanded music library.

161. Stoeckel Hall, when it was known as York Hall

162. Weir Courtyard

163. Old Art Gallery, on the corner of Chapel and High Streets

Weir Hall (1924)

Weir Hall, used for many years by the department of architecture, was named for the first director of the School of the Fine Arts (later called the School of Art and Architecture). Both its name and use were a far cry from the original concept of a building on this site. The dream of George Douglas Miller dating from 1877 had been to build a replica of Oxford in the heart of New Haven. He was the first to develop such a scheme at Yale, and he envisaged it as a dormitory for a senior society, Skull and Bones. His money ran out, however, before it could be completed, and there was scant interest on the part of the Society. The eventual rebuilding in 1965, while incorporating Weir into Jonathan Edwards College, provided for the Robert A. Taft Library and offices for college Fellows, and thus approached Mr. Miller's objective of a serene spot for contemplation "amid the city's jar."

The Old Art Gallery (1928)

The third art gallery to be built at Yale is connected with its predecessor, Street Hall, by a bridge over High Street. It contains a sculpture hall, a lecture room, offices for the department of the history of art, and studios in the tower. On the third floor are the Jarves Collection of early Italian art, the Trumbull Collection of Revolutionary War scenes and portraits of its principal participants, the Garvan collection of early American furniture and silver, and archeological findings from Dura-Europos.

164. The sculpture court of the old Art Gallery, facing the wall which now opens into the new gallery

and drama,

165. The audience gathers for a Drama School production

The School of Drama (1925/26)

The University Theatre was erected for the new department of drama, which became a School in 1955. It was the finest college theatrical complex of its day. The stage has the proportions of a professional theatre, and the auditorium provides for almost 700. The electronic switchboard, designed by George Izenour, performs miracles of intricate lighting effects at the touch of a finger. Similarly the ingenious use of modern mechanics has solved such problems as shifting 3,000 pounds of stage property in minutes. The theatre also includes lecture rooms, workshops for scenery, costumes, several rehearsal rooms, and an experimental theatre. The building has offices and a Green Room for social events as well. Each of these facilities has been carefully designed with a separate access from the theatre. Productions include original plays by students and a wide range of classical and contemporary drama, staged in both traditional and experimental styles – all open to the public. Books relating to the theatre were originally shelved in the Green Room, but in 1957 an addition was built to provide space for the 20,000-volume Theatre Library, which includes the personal library of the drama department's first chairman, Professor George Pierce Baker, and the Yale–Rockefeller Collection of 80,000 theatrical prints and photographs. The Crawford Collection of Modern Drama remains in Sterling Memorial Library. Rooms in the southwest corner of the building serve the undergraduate "Dramat."

166. Yale University Theatre at night, Tennessee Williams' "Camino Real" within

167. Mural and dinosaurs inside the Peabody Museum

Peabody Museum of Natural History (1923/24)

This museum, replacing the earlier one on Elm Street, commemorates George Peabody, a benefactor of both Yale and Harvard in the 19th century. While taking a cure for the gout at Wiesbaden in 1863, Mr. Peabody communicated to his nephew, O. C. Marsh the pioneer paleontologist, his intention to donate a considerable sum to Yale, "to promote the interests of *Natural Science* in that Institution." This gift produced the first Peabody Museum in 1876. The present brownstone building, designed in a French Gothic style, was the first museum in the United States to arrange its exhibits in biological and evolutionary order. In the Dinosaur Hall, the great mural by Rudolph Zallinger entitled "The Age of Reptiles" reconstructs that prehistoric era; a similar mural, "The Age of Mammals," spans the south wall of the Hall of Mammalian Evolution. Distinctive dioramas of North American animal life are other popular attractions viewed by over 170,000 visitors each year. Electronic Escorts, available in the museum, make individual tours an instructive occurrence. As a teaching museum, Peabody maintains a School Service Department which serves the Connecticut schools; the Peabody Museum Associates, organized in 1960, is responsible for the publication of *Discovery,* issued semi-annually, which describes the varied research expeditions of the staff and other aspects of the museum's scholarly activities.

168. Peabody Museum soon after it was built

There's always the need for dormitories and classrooms.

169. Wright Hall Court today

170. 1914 seniors gather by the lion in Wright Court

Wright Memorial Hall (1912)

Long an advocate of increasing dormitory facilities, Henry Parks Wright, Professor of Latin and first Dean of Yale College (1884–1909), was able in retirement to see this five-story building erected in his honor in 1912, the gift of generations of Yale men and their families. Alumni Hall occupied this site before Wright Hall was built, and it was a happy choice to place Wright Hall here, with its many reminders of those who had met to debate, take examinations, attend lectures, and organize clubs in the "shortest, gladdest years of life." The basement of Wright houses Yale Station, facilities for the distribution of inter-office mail, and the Housekeeping Department. The telephone exchange is in the basement and the first floor. The Daniels Memorial Gateway was erected between Wright and Durfee in 1912.

William L. Harkness Hall (1927)

A gift from Mr. Harkness (a cousin of Edward S. Harkness), supplemented by funds from his widow and children, provided sorely needed classroom space. Harkness Hall also contains a lecture hall, faculty offices for English, history, and modern languages, and the office of the University's Alumni Records. Adjacent to Sprague Hall on two sides, it was the first building to define the Cross Campus on the east side of Blount Avenue. Calhoun and Berkeley colleges now complete the design, which was conceived to provide a suitable frame for Sterling Memorial Library.

171. William L. Harkness Hall. The students protest on behalf of a favorite professor

172. McClellan Hall, right, and Connecticut, left

173. "Yale Campus in Here (occupied)": McClellan's construction met with widespread criticism

Edwin McClellan Hall (1925)

This building caused a stir when efficient contractors started excavating before President Angell could inform the Yale community. Students were outraged and the faculty were upset. It was explained that the building would relieve the dormitory shortage and the design, a free version of Connecticut Hall, would add to the symmetry of the Old Campus. The proposed building was quickly labeled "Hush Hall," and this epithet, with the slogan, "For God, for Country, and for Symmetry" were painted on the fence around the excavation. Another section had the words:
The Faculty's frantic, the students are wild
For Mother Connecticut's having a child!
Work was resumed after two hectic months, and students staged a "Pageant of Symmetry" at the laying of the cornerstone.

Charles W. Bingham Hall (1928)

Bingham Hall, the third Yale building to occupy the site on the corner of Chapel and College Streets, was completed in 1928. This most recent Freshman dormitory is entered through the '96 Memorial Gateway to the Old Campus or through a walk between Bingham and Vanderbilt. The tower houses the Palmer-Schreiber German Library and a small planetarium. Commemorative bas-reliefs record the location of Yale College and the old Fence.

174. Charles W. Bingham Hall, c. 1930

175. Handsome Dan IX

176. Yale Field, with Walter Camp Gateway in the foreground

Yale Bowl (1913/14)

The first game was played in the Yale Bowl on November 21, 1914, against Harvard: Yale lost 36–0. But New Haven had never seen such a weekend. When, in 1908, it was clear that the old Yale Field's capacity of 35,000 was inadequate, a committee of twenty-one graduates was selected to make plans for the new athletic fields. They proposed a new football field, baseball stands, a field house, and ample room for undergraduate intramural athletics. They also agreed that the University itself should have no part in raising so large an athletic fund. In the hope of making the stadium as large and as safe as possible, the unique idea of scooping the bowl out of the ground was conceived; the playing field and half the stands are below ground level. Early in Bowl history, Yale classes marched to the field to cheer the team, and until 1947 many spectators arrived at football games on open trolleys. After his death in 1899, the original Yale mascot, Handsome Dan, a regular attendant at all athletic events, was stuffed and placed in the Trophy Room of the Gymnasium. The present mascot is Handsome Dan X.

The Walter Camp Gateway (1927/28)

The Walter Camp Gateway, leading into Yale Feld, is a national memorial to the father of American football. The funds for its construction were donated by 503 schools and colleges throughout the country.

177. Taking a coach to the Yale–Princeton football game in 1889. Result: Yale 10, Princeton 0

and athletes practiced here.

178. The Yale Armory

179. Lapham Field House and tennis courts

180. An afternoon drill in old Artillery Hall, with seniors in charge

181. Polo in the Armory

Yale Armory

The Armory, completed in 1917, was designed for Yale's Army ROTC, the first such program in the country. The building near the Yale Bowl was originally divided into drill hall, gun sheds, and stables. Plans for an armory were initiated by President Hadley, an advocate of military preparedness, who instituted military training at Yale in 1915 and organized the Yale Artillery Battalion in 1916. When World War I came, Yale had 8,000 men in the service; five per cent of all the artillery officers were Yale men. The Armory was said to be the finest artillery training site outside of Fort Sill, and the University was given four 75-millimeter cannons by the French government for training purposes. By the winter of 1918, only 200 undergraduates on the campus were not in uniform. Many had left for training elsewhere, and 2,400 were training at Yale. Soon the campus was crowded with regular Army volunteers attending training sessions. The Armory is now used for indoor polo, a rifle range, and dressing rooms.

Charles E. Coxe Memorial Gymnasium (1927)

More commonly called Coxe Cage, this building with facilities for indoor track and baseball was to be used for winter conditioning of spring teams. It can also be adapted for tennis courts. The Cage was built when the University was hoping to discourage the idea that athletics were only for members of varsity teams.

182. Coxe Cage

183. The Adee Boat House

184. The Faculty Club

185. The Graduate Club

Faculty Club (1764–67)

The Faculty Club was purchased by the University from Secretary Stokes, who had lived there since 1900. When the British occupied New Haven in 1779, they used this house as a hospital; when Mr. Stokes lived there, the Yale Foreign Missionary Society ("Yale-in-China") and the Connecticut Society for Mental Hygiene were organized in the "Keeping Room." The building has served as a social headquarters for faculty families since 1922. Restored to its 18th-century appearance in 1929, the building has furnishings supplemented with many pieces from Yale's Garvan Collection of Early American Furniture. An addition was built in memory of President Angell in 1957.

Graduate Club (1799)

Long known as the Whitney Blake House, this building facing the Green was acquired for the Graduate Club Association in 1901. Alumni of all accredited colleges and universities are eligible for membership.

Elizabethan Club (ca. 1810–15)

The Elizabethan Club occupies a distinguished old Federal house on College Street. "The Lizzie," celebrated in song by Cole Porter, '13, grew during the literary renaissance at the University between 1909 and 1920 and soon fostered collector's fever with the encouragement of William Lyon Phelps, Chauncey Tinker, and John Berdan. Its library contains Elizabethan folios and quartos and many early engravings and paintings.

186. The Elizabethan Club

187. An Elizabethan Club play, 1915

188. The Lizzie vault

especially at Mory's.

189. Mory's on Temple Street celebrates the Bicentennial, 1901

Mory's

En route from races on the harbor, members of the Class of 1863 discovered an ale house on Wooster Street operated by a Mr. and Mrs. Moriarty. It soon became so popular that the proprietors moved it to Court Street, where it maintained the same atmosphere and became known as "The Quiet House." In 1876 the widow moved to Temple Street and became the mistress of Temple Bar; here Louis Linder presided from 1898. The Moriartys were not forgotten, and their name lives on in the association formed in 1912 by alumni as a private club. A wooden house formerly occupied by faculty families (including Dean – later Governor – Wilbur L. Cross) and resembling the Temple Bar building was purchased, and Mory's was established. The Whiffenpoofs, composed of the Varsity Quartet plus a fifth singer, harmonized first at the Temple Bar.

191. Mory's moved in 1912 to its present York Street site

190. A carved table

192. Whiffenpoofs in Mory's, 1935

Buildings of Yale: 1929–1952

Buildings in black, which were built or acquired by Yale in this period,
appear in Part IV.
Buildings in gray were built earlier but were still standing at this time.
The street grid is New Haven of 1966.

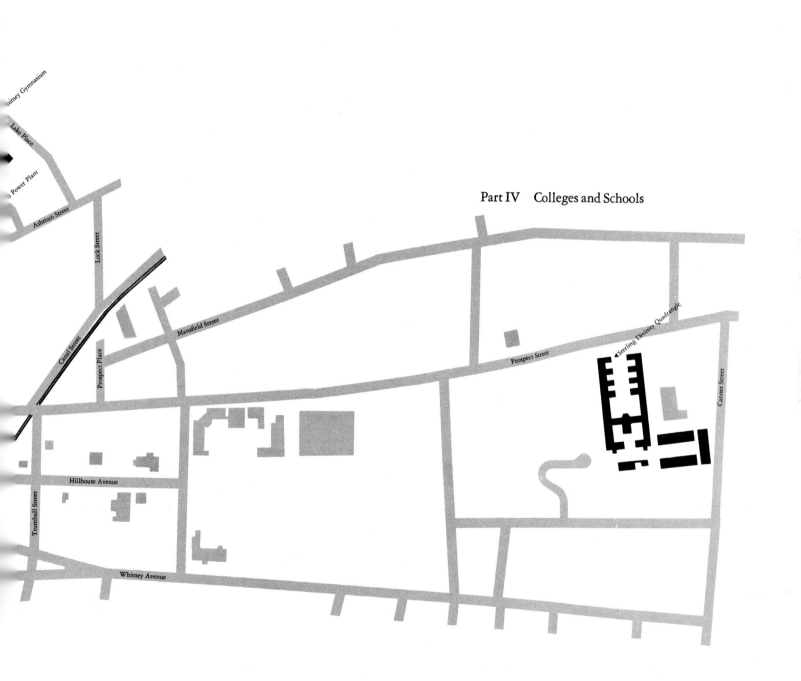

Part IV   Colleges and Schools

Colleges within Colleges gave life to

193. The Old Campus in the snow. Freshmen living here take part in the activities of their residential colleges, and they move to the colleges at the beginning
of the sophomore year

194. The Trumbull Room in Branford College

195. Linonia Court, James Fenimore Cooper Entry, Branford

Branford College (1933)

Although the original Yale buildings on the Old Brick Row were called "colleges," the name and model taken from Oxford and Cambridge, it was not until the first third of this century that the entire idea of residential colleges was realized. Branford was remodeled from the Memorial Quadrangle to become the first of the residential colleges. Five floors of student rooms in the Branford section were removed to create a dining hall and a common room; other student rooms were sacrificed to make way for libraries and living quarters for the Master and for the Resident Fellows. The gates between Branford and Saybrook, kept locked in order to create separate identities, are opened at reunion time and for the Senior Prom. For many years the Senior Class Day Exercises at graduation were held in Branford court, often called the most beautiful college quadrangle in America. As the graduating class grew, the ceremony was moved to the Old Campus, but it is still a Branford tradition to stay off the grass until Commencement. Three other courts, Linonia (seen here), Calliopean, and Brothers in Unity, provide respite from the noise of the city. At the base of Harkness Tower is the College Chapel.

196. Branford Court and Wrexham Tower

197. A concert in Saybrook's court

198. The early wooden gates open into Saybrook

Saybrook College (1933)

Saybrook forms the side of the Memorial Quadrangle on Elm Street, between High and York. Its two courtyards are named for towns that figured in early Yale history. In Saybrook the first classes were held; in Killingworth Rector Pierson conducted his own classes. It was from Killingworth that an ancient millstone was brought by oxen in 1921 and set in Killingworth Court. Both courts are rich in sculpture, and the entryways all bear the names of distinguished graduates. They provide a setting for concerts, buffet dinners, student dances and parties, and Commencement ceremonies. At Commencement, each college forms a procession, with a banner bearer, Master, Dean, Fellows, and students, and makes its way to the Old Campus. After the formal exercises, they return to their individual colleges, where they personally receive from the Master their diploma and a certificate of their own college. Each college has about 250 students, most of whom room with two other classmates in suites consisting of a living room and two bedrooms. Although they live on the Old Campus, Freshmen are now affiliated with the colleges and have the opportunity to participate in their programs.

199. The Killingworth stone on its way to Saybrook College

200. The stone in place in Killingworth Court

201. The stone in Killingworth, Connecticut

202. Trumbull students prepare for the annual Beer and Bike Race

Trumbull College (1929/33)

The dormitory units called Sterling Quadrangle were renamed Trumbull College, and a library, common room, master's house, and dining hall were added when the college plan came into effect. The college was named after a Governor of both the colony and state of Connecticut, Jonathan Trumbull, who was known as "Brother Jonathan" by George Washington. It has three courts; the dining hall forms the southern border of the central court, and the Sterling Memorial Library reading room forms the northern border. Trumbull men are called Bulls, a name taken from the college's arms. Along with a coat of arms, each of Yale's twelve colleges has its own design for silverware and china, a banner carried in official processions, and a specially created bookplate. A unique feature of residential college life is the Bursary System, which was endowed by Mr. Harkness when he gave his colleges. This program provides jobs for students who are on scholarship or those who need financial help. Although the bursary students are employed by the University, they often work in their own colleges. Here they serve as librarians, athletic secretaries, and as office assistants. A Senior is designated Chief Aide; he is responsible to the master and college dean and is in charge of organizing the student staff.

203. A view of the York Street court of Trumbull College

204. Pierson Courtyard

205. Inside the Pierson dining hall

Pierson College (1931)

Named after the first President (or Rector) of Yale, Pierson was the first college to be built under the residential college plan with the gift from Edward S. Harkness. Pierson, built in Georgian Colonial style, fronts on York Street but is separated by a long walkway and secluded from the noise of the city. The Pierson dining hall recalls the interior of an old New England meeting house. But as in all the colleges the atmosphere is generally casual, with enough formality to promote respectability: students are required to wear coats and ties. The small, low-gabled, white-painted court, reminiscent of white-washed slave quarters, gives Piersonians their name, the Slaves. The college seminars, originally designed for sophomores and now including students from all classes, are taught by Fellows of the colleges and cover virtually all fields of study. Pierson normally has five or six seminars, involving 12 students in each. Freshmen who are eager to begin concentrating in a special field are offered semi-tutorial seminars. Each of these is affiliated with one of the colleges and taught by a Fellow of that college. In addition, distinguished visitors, traditionally in the field of literature or foreign affairs, speak at the college.

206. The "Slave Quarters" of Pierson

Hybrids,

207. Davenport's Queen Anne "rear" can be seen from the court

Davenport College (1933)

John Davenport, a founder of the New Haven Colony was a distinguished preacher and one of the first to propose a college here. Cotton Mather's Latin epitaph to Davenport, inscribed on the north terrace, has the following free translation:

Up to heaven as he ort,
Went the Reverend Davenport
Church's and New England's pride,
All mourned sadly when he died.

Davenport's Gothic exterior was planned to blend with the Memorial Quadrangle across York Street. The Colonial Georgian courtyard, however, fits well with Pierson College. As a result of this meshing of architectural forms, the men of Davenport have been called Hybrids. Athletic rivalries between Davenport and Pierson customarily rose to fever pitch on the evening before the Davenport-Pierson game, when the men of Pierson, parading into the Davenport court to announce their impending victory, were doused with gallons of water; the gates had been locked to make a quick exit impossible. Davenport has four or five Resident Fellows, who make themselves available for seminars and student counseling and assist the Master in a variety of ways. One of them is usually the College Dean, who is in charge of academic life and discipline.

208. Davenport's Gothic façade, on view from York Street

Senators,

209. A 1942 student production of "All's Well that Ends Well"

210. Festival of the Arts in 1963

Calhoun College (1932)

This college is named for John C. Calhoun, a graduate of the Class of 1804, Senator from South Carolina, and Vice-President of the United States. It is arranged around one large court, which is built on several levels. In the buildings are many mementoes of Calhoun: a portrait and bust, the windows of the common room with scenes of Calhoun as statesman and farmer, and Currier and Ives prints of the life of the Southern gentleman during Calhoun's time. The members of Calhoun have been nicknamed the Senators, and the Senator's birthday provides the excuse for an annual celebration. The Calhoun Players, an informal dramatic group, traditionally produces one Shakespearean play each spring, with the stage effectively improvised in the dining hall. Calhoun, like the other residential colleges, has a debating team, several publications, and its own orchestra (depending on current talent). Each year the residential colleges join in a week-long Arts Festival. Students show paintings and produce musical and dramatic works. The college's location on the corner of Elm and College Streets was cause for anxiety when streetcars rounded the corner every few minutes. Today the very absence of this din is the cause of celebration, an annual autumn party known as "Trolley Night."

211. Calhoun from the Cross Campus

212. Beekman Cannon and Mrs. Beecher Hogan perform at a Gottschalk Concert

Jonathan Edwards College (1932)

Jonathan Edwards, minister, theologian, philosopher, naturalist, one of America's foremost colonial thinkers, member of the Class of 1720, and Yale tutor, wrote a respected treatise on spiders when he was fourteen. The spider web is found on the china of Jonathan Edwards College, its men are called "Spiders," and the concern of Edwards for original sin is symbolized by the college badge, an apple surrounded by a snake. The college incorporates two older dormitories, Wheelock and Dickinson Halls, with new buildings including a dormitory on High Street, the common rooms, a library, dining hall, kitchens, and the master's house. It has also annexed most of Weir Hall, which is used principally for the College's Robert A. Taft Library. The potpourri of architectural styles gives Jonathan Edwards an irregular, picturesque air. Intellectual and cultural programs abound in J.E.: seminars and concerts, Gilbert and Sullivan operettas, and exhibitions. A long-standing tradition is the Victorian evening of musical and dramatic satire, staged by the Fellows and their wives. A special college fund provides assistance to students who want to attend musical events in New Haven and New York. J.E. was also one of the first colleges to have a printing press.

213. Croquet in J.E. Court

214. Inside the new Robert A. Taft Library

215. The dining hall

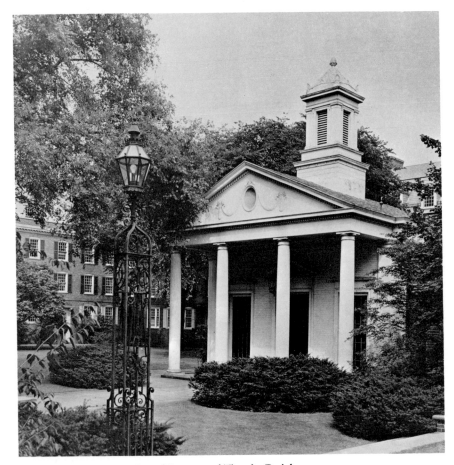

216. The hall entrance to the public rooms of Timothy Dwight

Timothy Dwight College (1934)

Timothy Dwight, the College of Presidents, was named for two Yale Presidents: Timothy Dwight the elder, Class of 1769, President from 1795 to 1817, and his grandson, Timothy Dwight the younger, Class of 1849, President from 1866 to 1899. Members of the College have been nicknamed Prexies after the namesakes, and in recent years Fellows of Timothy Dwight have also included Yale Presidents Griswold and Brewster. The Federal architecture is reminiscent of the period of the elder Timothy Dwight. The college living quarters, like those in the Old Campus and most of the other colleges, are designed around entries of four floors; each floor has two suites accommodating six to ten students. The entries are connected in all the colleges by a basement or underground tunnels. Timothy Dwight College sponsors the Chubb Fellowship program, endowed by Hendon Chubb, Ph.B. 1895, for the purpose of creating better understanding of the problems of government. It brings to the college congressmen, senators, governors, and diplomats, who live in the college during this period and mingle with the students in classrooms, the dining hall, and after-dinner conversations. A similar program annually brings men of arts and letters to the college.

217. Harry S. Truman, Chubb Fellow, and Messrs Lee, Bergin, Ribicoff, and Acheson

218. Barry Goldwater, Chubb Fellow, April 1962

220. Robert Wagner, April 1966

219. Adlai Stevenson, Chubb Fellow, in Master's sitting room, April 1959

221. Iris Murdoch, T.D. Fellow in Arts and Letters, 1959

Mitres,

222. A seminar in the Swiss Room in Berkeley

223. The Lounge

Berkeley College (1934)

Berkeley College was built on the site of the old Berkeley Oval, and it was originally intended that the Oval would be remade, like the Harkness Quadrangle, into a college or two. But James Gamble Rogers, the architect, balked at this because he felt that the Oval buildings detracted from the view of the new library. The plan of two new courts, the open ends facing the Cross Campus, with a tunnel to connect the two wings, was chosen as a workable solution. The courts provide a broad, grassy, and inviting approach to the Sterling Memorial Library. The collegiate Gothic style conforms with the surrounding Calhoun College and William L. Harkness Hall. The dining hall and common rooms have open timber roofs reminiscent of Tudor Gothic. The walls of the Swiss Room, used as a Fellows' Common Room and for seminars and student functions, are actually made up of two panelled rooms from Switzerland dating from about the year 1500. One of the special annual events of the College is the celebration of Bishop Berkeley's Birthday, complete with cake, academic gowns, and "tar water." Trainees in the World War II Army Specialized Training Program were housed in Berkeley. They could be heard counting cadence as they walked to Freshman Commons.

224. Soldiers of World War II Army Specialized Training Program line up in front of Berkeley

and Salamanders.

225. Silliman courtyard, Grove Street entrance

Silliman College (1940)

Benjamin Silliman, B.A. 1796, the first professor of chemistry at Yale and also a famous geologist, was instrumental in the founding of the Yale School of Medicine in 1813, the *American Journal of Science* in 1818, the Art Gallery, the Sheffield Scientific School, and the Peabody Museum. The college named after this great innovator at Yale was opened in 1940. The last of the original cluster of residential colleges, it is the largest college, with an average student population of 413; planners felt a large college on this site was economically wiser than two smaller ones. It incorporated the Vanderbilt-Scientific dormitories and Byers Hall. Today the Van-Sheff section on College Street houses law students. Byers Hall contains the common rooms, music room, library, and several Fellows' suites. The new buildings, constructed between 1938 and 1940, are Georgian and, unlike similar Yale buildings, have no shutters. One of the most highly praised features of Silliman was the inclusion of the first women's powder room, now a regular facility in all colleges. The symbol of Silliman is the salamander, because of its ancient association with fire and the sciences, and the members of the college have come to be called "Salamanders."

226. Silliman Court

From all over the world came graduate students

227. Foreign students congregate in the lounge of the Hall of Graduate Studies

The Graduate School (1932)

The idea of graduate education was part of Ezra Stiles' dream of a University, although it was not for many years that formal graduate education was a part of Yale. President Timothy Dwight put the first touches to Stiles' dream by laying the foundations for the professional schools of the traditional Continental university – medicine, law, and divinity. In 1861 Yale conferred its first Ph.D., the first to be given by any University in the United States. Homes for the graduate school during the early years were many and usually inadequate. The first headquarters was a shabby frame building on High Street near the old Peabody Museum. The building also stored inflammable materials, and Dean Wilbur Cross objected to the danger inherent in these quarters. The Graduate School then moved into Addison Van Name's former home and there remained until the Sterling donation made the modern building possible. At the time of building it was the most complete to be devoted to graduate study anywhere, although today it can accommodate but a fraction of the school's bursting enrollment. Yale's graduate school now grants advanced degrees in 54 fields. It also combines work with such schools as Medicine, Law, Divinity, Forestry, and Music. The Master of Arts in Teaching program was added in 1954 for secondary school teachers. In 1966 a new degree, the Master of Philosophy, was devised to satisfy the pressing need for college teachers.

228. Where the graduate students eat

229. A view into the small court, Hall of Graduate Studies

to the cathedral-like library,

230. Main reading room, Sterling Memorial Library

Sterling Memorial Library (1930)

In his will John W. Sterling expressed the wish that some monumental building should commemorate him, and the Corporation agreed that the University Library should have this distinction. It took four years to build, and, in style and ornament, resembles a Gothic cathedral. It has a sixteen-story stack tower and all public reading rooms and departments are on the main floor; the approaches to the circulation desk contain exhibition cases for rotating display of Yale treasures. In the baronial nave, a decorative frieze depicts the history of Yale and its library. The central courtyard is a popular warm-weather refuge for students. Adjacent to the court is Linonia and Brothers Library, and on the other side of the main entrance is the Reserve Book Room and the Yale College Library of 1742. Other special collections include the holdings and offices of the American Oriental Society, the private papers of James Boswell, the Horace Walpole Collection, the notably complete material on Benjamin Franklin and his times, and the Yale Achives. Scholars in fields represented by collections advise the library staff about accessions. Sterling Memorial Library contains approximately two-thirds of the nearly 5,000,000 volumes of university holdings, the balance being distributed in The Beinecke Rare Book and Manuscript Library, professional schools, and departmental libraries.

231. A rooftop view

232. The Savage mural behind the call desk

233. A view of the library

234. Entering the library

235. The Anthony N. Brady Memorial Laboratory, School of Medicine

School of Medicine (1924)
School of Nursing (1952)

The third location of the School of Medicine brought it partially onto property of what was then the New Haven Hospital. Although the two institutions were independently controlled, affiliation developed gradually as new concepts of medical teaching were advanced. The first building to be designed as an outpatient clinic was given to the University in 1901 and named the Jane Ellen Hope Memorial. Brady Memorial Laboratory, completed in 1917, was the first of the more modern buildings. Enlarged in 1928, it now houses the offices of the School of Nursing, which offers the degree of Master of Science in Nursing. The Sterling Hall of Medicine, erected in 1924, was planned to provide locations for the clinical departments in close association with the hospital wards. This administrative center of the Medical School has been altered and expanded several times. In 1929–30 the façade was changed to make it continuous with the Institute of Human Relations, a building in which revolutionary concepts of interdisciplinary studies in the social sciences were inaugurated. The Mary S. Harkness Memorial Auditorium was added in 1960/61; the most extensive addition was the Yale Medical Library, completed in 1941. Lauder Hall is contiguous to Brady, and Farnam Memorial Buildings were built in 1928 and have since been enlarged and expanded.

236. The Institute of Human Relations

237. The Medical School from the garden

238. The main entrance

239. The Sterling Hall of Medicine looked like this between 1925 and 1929

240. Inside Marquand Chapel

Divinity School (1928)

The Sterling Divinity Quadrangle perpetuates the architectural tradition of 18th-century New England, although the general arrangement is modeled on Jefferson's University of Virginia. The Quadrangle, one of the most picturesque and secluded areas of the university, contains quarters for 160 men, a chapel, a recitation building, an administration building, a library building, common rooms, a gymnasium, and two guest lodges. The housing units of the Quadrangle are named for distinguished ministers, theologians, and missionaries who were graduates of Yale: Hopkins, Brainerd, Seabury, Beecher, Taylor, Bacon, and Bushnell. Additional facilities to house married and women students, with a dean's house, were completed in 1957. Although Yale's origin was Congregational, the School maintains an interdenominational character. Its faculty includes most Protestant denominations as well as members of the Roman Catholic faith. Most graduates become ministers, but the curriculum provides training in six areas: pastoral, missionary, Christian education, community service, religious leadership in colleges and universities, and teaching and research in religion. Under the auspices of the Graduate School, a Department of Religious Studies offers a Ph.D. in the history of religions and general theological studies.

241. Student quarters

242. Marquand Chapel

243. The Sterling Divinity Quadrangle

244. The way into the Law School

Law School (1931)

Yale's approach to law arises from the philosophy that the law is a process of historical change. The School has pioneered in looking at law as an instrument of social policy; students are encouraged to look beyond the legal aspects to history, philosophy, and the social sciences. Action and participation are not divorced from the principles that are the subject of classroom study and debate, and Yale students and faculty take part in the social and intellectual issues of the time.

The Sterling Law Buildings, erected in 1934, were designed to recall the English Inns of Court and are richly embellished with genre sculpture and stained-glass medallions. The stonework around the outside of the building depicts processes of the law in the form of gargoyles: a policeman apprehending a burglar, a judge passing sentence, a convict in stripes contemplating his own crime, a convict cracking stone, a lawyer as a parrot, a judge as an owl. The quadrangle, occupying an entire city block, includes offices, seminar rooms, library, courtrooms, classrooms, an auditorium, faculty and student lounges, dining hall, and the residential accommodations for male students. Such facilities are a far cry from the School's humble beginnings in New Haven private offices and the city hall. The building is connected to the Sterling Library by a tunnel, and an addition to the Law Library is built underground next to The Beinecke Rare Book and Manuscript Library.

245. Distinguished justices sit on the court for the Stone Prize Argument

246. Swearing in at Moot Court

247. Law School lounge and dining hall

248. An interior court

249. The Payne Whitney Gymnasium on Tower Parkway

Payne Whitney Gymnasium (1930/32)
Ray Tompkins House (1931/32)

The central portion or tower of the Payne Whitney Gymnasium, located on Tower Parkway, contains rowing tanks, basketball courts, practice pools, locker rooms, rooms for boxing, wrestling, and fencing, a trophy room, and offices. The right wing has the basketball amphitheatre, squash courts, and a running track. The left wing contains the exhibition swimming pool and handball courts. Every freshman participates in some form of athletic activity during his first term at Yale. This can, of course, include formal freshman sports. The 2,187 seats in the exhibition pool rise steeply toward the ceiling and provide spectators with an unobstructed view of the pool. The Ray Tompkins House provides offices for the University Athletic Association, rooms for visiting teams, a lounge, and training table.

Department of University Health (1929/30)

Health facilities were first housed in the second gymnasium under the direction of a physician, and students were examined and their measurements taken at entrance and graduation. These duties were transferred in 1916 to the new Department of University Health. The present building was completed in 1930. Mrs. Timothy Dwight was responsible for securing donations for an Infirmary, which was completed on Prospect Street in 1892. Mrs. Charles P. Taft provided a subsequent addition.

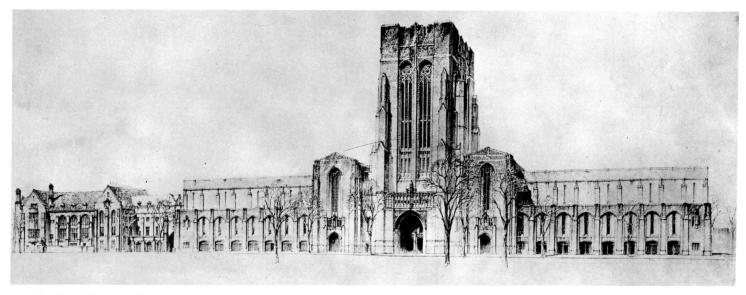

250. John Russell Pope's rendering of Ray Tompkins House and the gymnasium

251. Rowing tank practice

252. Department of University Health

253. The University Heating and Power Plant

254. Sheffield Hall, Sterling Tower, and Strathcona Hall

University Heating and Power Plant (1918)

When the Memorial Quadrangle was being planned, the need for modern equipment for heating and lighting was clear. This building was designed to match the collegiate gothic style of the Quadrangle. The department of business management is in the building next door.

Sheffield-Sterling-Strathcona Hall (1931/32)

The names of this composite building commemorate donors to the University. Sheffield Hall contains offices of the Dean of Yale College, classrooms, and the Aurelian Honor Society. Sterling Tower houses the Registrar's office, conference rooms, and a faculty lounge. Strathcona has a large lecture hall. Rooms above the hall (formerly the Torch Honor Society) are now used by the Scholars of the House program, the Senior Advisory Board, and other student activities.

The Briton Hadden Memorial Building: The *Yale Daily News* (1931/32)

The *News* was founded in 1878 and has been published continuously throughout the college year, except during wartime. Opportunity to "heel" the *News* is open to all students in good standing; the lively articles which the editorial board sponsors reflect undergraduate opinion and sentiment in uncensored variety. The *News* also publishes a "Course Critique," with candid analyses of instructors and course content.

255. The Briton Hadden Memorial Building

Buildings of Yale: 1953–1966

Buildings in black, which were built or acquired by Yale in this period,
appear in Part V.
Buildings in gray were built earlier but were still standing at this time.
The street grid is New Haven of 1966.

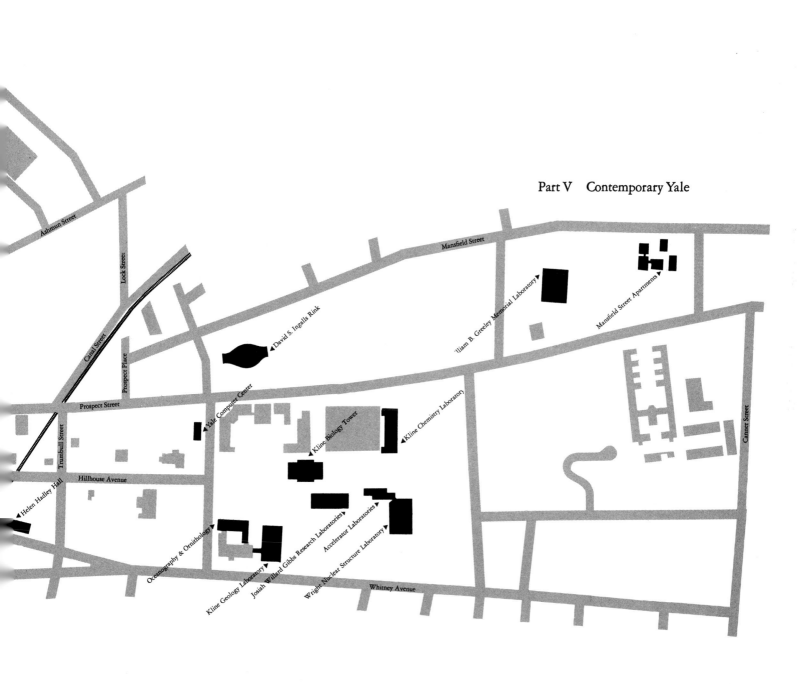

Part V   Contemporary Yale

Ashmun Street

Lock Street

Canal Street

Mansfield Street

Prospect Place

Prospect Street

David S. Ingalls Rink

'Iiam B. Greeley Memorial Laboratory ▶

Mansfield Street Apartments ▶

Canner Street

Yale Computer Center

Kline Biology Tower

Kline Chemistry Laboratory ◀

Trumbull Street

Hillhouse Avenue

Helen Hadley Hall ◀

Oceanography & Ornithology ▶

Kline Geology Laboratory ◀

Josiah Willard Gibbs Research Laboratories ▶

Accelerator Laboratories ▶

Wright Nuclear Structure Laboratory ▶

Whitney Avenue

256. Weir Court view of the Art Gallery. The top floor was then used by architecture students

257. Interior of the Art Gallery, showing sculptures once in the old Art Gallery wing

New Art Gallery (1953)

This extensive addition to the Art Gallery was designed in brick and glass by Louis Kahn. It was the first building of Yale's new architectural era under the Griswold administration, and Yale now moved toward leadership in contemporary academic architecture. The building became a landmark because of its new use of space, experimental tetrahedron ceilings, and movable exhibition partitions. First known as the Art Gallery and Design Center, it included the department of architecture, facilities for graphic arts, and extensions of the earlier gallery. With the completion of the neighboring building devoted entirely to the School of Art and Architecture, the Gallery was released for exhibition space. Its four floors and lower level are used for exhibitions, offices, and workrooms. It adjoins the Old Gallery, and to the north has an outdoor sculpture court which faces on Weir Hall. Although the Yale Gallery is in effect a municipal museum, its primary purposes are associated with the University's teaching and research at the graduate, undergraduate, and professional levels. Because of this, no special effort has been made to build up a large collection of works of art by any one artist. The Gallery concentrates on one or two important examples of many important artists and schools.

258. Chapel Street view of Art Gallery; old Art Gallery on far right and School of Art and Architecture on the left

259. Fourth floor and fifth floor mezzanine, with Minerva watching

260. Sewell Sillman painting his mural on the fifth floor mezzanine

Art and Architecture Building (1963)

The new home of the School of Art and Architecture, by the former chairman of the architecture department, Paul Rudolph, provides classrooms, offices, studios, and an auditorium for the teaching programs in painting, architecture, city planning, sculpture, graphic design, and print-making, a large library used by the historians of art, and a suite for visiting critics and scholars. Here, for the first time in Yale history, all cognate facilities in the art area have been brought together under one roof. The building is made of a hammered concrete aggregate, producing a corrugated surface both inside and out; glass is used on all of the nine stories, which actually include 36 different levels. All levels depend on natural light. *Architectural Forum* commented on the design and its function: "Ceilings soar or suddenly descend near head level; each room is as if invented as a new kind of space. . . . The building will challenge, disturb, and possibly inspire the students within it. . . . Education in America needs more shock treatment, not less." The growing recognition of and concern for the arts have already made these quarters inadequate in size. Many painting classes have been obliged to find space in other University buildings, and the critical relationship of city planning to other academic fields has given it new priority in the University's programs for the future.

261. The Art and Architecture School

262. The Ingalls Rink from above

263. The entrance to the Ingalls Rink

David S. Ingalls Rink (1957/58)

This 3,000-seat arena was conceived by Eero Saarinen and constructed of concrete with an aluminum roof suspended by cables from a central arch. In addition to varsity and freshman hockey, it is used for intramural games, and by the faculty, their families, and students. The rink can also accommodate 6,000 people for rainy day Commencement or Class Day exercises. Hockey had long lacked adequate facilities of its own. Teams first played on an open-air rink at Yale Field, and from 1900 until the completion of Ingalls Rink, they leased commercial arenas in the city. Art historian Vincent Scully describes the roof of the building as being "draped tent-like from the center beam. The effect is that the roof is a plastic shell over a building that comes up swimming out of the earth. The upward curve of the arch inside suggests and expresses the sweeping rushes of hockey itself." During construction the Rink was dubbed the "turtle," then the "whale." These epithets did not bother Saarinen. "What intrigues me most," he said, "is to imagine archaeologists 5,000 years from now digging in New Haven and first coming across the Peabody Museum, and then not so far away from there finding this huge dinosaur-like skeleton. What kind of history will they reconstruct about the kind of formidable creatures Yale men were in this twentieth century!"

264. A hockey game

265. Sculpture and architecture harmonize in Ezra Stiles College

Ezra Stiles College (1960/62)

The construction of new residential colleges to relieve the postwar undergraduate overcrowding was given the highest priority in the 1950s. Yale College not only had a population of 200 more students than in the prewar years, but four students now had to live in the former two-man suites. In 1955, John Hay Whitney made it possible for Yale to purchase the New Haven High School properties which had long divided the campus between the Hall of Graduate Studies and the Payne Whitney Gymnasium. Three years later, the Old Dominion Foundation, founded by Paul Mellon, gave the University a large grant, half to be employed for the construction of two new colleges and half for the permanent endowment of college-centered educational activities in all twelve residential colleges. The new units, designed by Eero Saarinen, accommodate 250 students each. Ezra Stiles College was named after the President of Yale (1778–95), who was considered one of the most learned men of his time. The idea that the traditional styles of architecture should be maintained in the new colleges was quickly dispelled when Saarinen was appointed designer. In a remarkable sense the buildings he produced, but never lived to see, are in his words "good neighbors"; they do not clash in form or mass with the collegiate gothic structures beside them.

266. Nivola sculpts in concrete

267. Enjoying the sculpture

268. Ezra Stiles dining hall

269. An overall view of Ezra Stiles and Morse Colleges

270. The 1966 Senior Prom in the dining hall

271. "Spanish Steps" between Morse and Ezra Stiles

Morse College (1962)

When Eero Saarinen, the architect, was considering the design of the new colleges and the way in which they would blend with the Yale that was, he commented that "Yale could stand two or three more towers," and these he built after the manner of the north Italian village of San Gimignano, balancing the towers of the Hall of Graduate Studies, the Gymnasium, and Christ Church. The shape of the site inspired an arrangement of buildings in two semicircles set back to back, forming oddly shaped courtyards. Room was left to the north for a series of buildings to complete the mall in front of the Payne Whitney Gymnasium. The rough walls, jagged towers, irregular student rooms (the majority are singles), and the winding walkways are enhanced by the sculpture of Constantino Nivola. Morse is named after Samuel F. B. Morse, '10, called the "American Leonardo" because of his fame as a painter, inventor, teacher, and entrepreneur. The college newspaper is called the *Morse Telegraph.* Undergraduates may often be seen playing softball in the caverns of the college; the massive stone towers provide excellent backstops.

Yale Cooperative Corporation

When Ezra Stiles College was built, the "Co-op" also gained an adjacent new home, designed by Saarinen in the same style. This came 77 years after its founding as a one-room store in the Old Laboratory, run by a group of students and instructors.

272. The Morse College Library

273. The Yale Co-op

274. A student's room in Morse

and a library – an alabaster honeycomb.

The Beinecke Rare Book and Manuscript Library (1961/63)

Designed as a rectangular marble box, this library is the gift of the Beinecke family and the architectural creation of Gordon Bunshaft. Thought to be the largest building in the world reserved entirely for rare books and manuscripts, it has a capacity of over 800,000 volumes, and, in addition to the central tower, there are three floors of stacks under Hewitt Quadrangle, which surrounds the building. Among the special contents are the Yale collections of Western Americana, American literature, and medieval manuscripts. On exhibition in the temperature- and moisture-controlled cases on the ground and mezzanine floors are the Gutenberg Bible, the first book printed from movable type; the Vinland Map; Audubon's *Birds of America;* and a rotating selection of great manuscripts and printed books. The building itself seems to float on four small cones in the middle of the marble quadrangle. The translucent Vermont marble of the walls protects the books from direct sunlight but lets in some of the natural light which enhances the beauty of the ancient bindings in the central stacks. The Library is divided into three parts: the exhibition hall, the study areas, including the reading rooms, catalogue room, microfilm room, offices, and the book storage vaults. The sculptures in the sunken courtyard are by Noguchi and represent time – the pyramid, sun – the circle, and chance – the cube.

275. Translucent marble of the Beinecke Library surrounds the stack tower

276. The Beinecke Rare Book and Manuscript Library

Yale now has married students with children,

Quonset Huts

When the veterans, many of them married, began returning to the campus after World War II, the University hastily erected Quonset Huts; many survived far beyond expectation, and most tenants proved to be model housekeepers.

Mansfield Street Apartments (1960/61)

These apartments house 51 graduate married couples. Their unique design brought wide recognition to the architect, Paul Rudolph.

277. Graduate students were housed in quonset huts after World War II

278. Mansfield Street Apartments, for married graduate students

279. The children of married students at the playground, designed by Neil Welliver, outside Mansfield Street Apartments

and quiet spots to watch stars and place asterisks.

280. Helen Hadley Hall, for women graduate students

Helen Hadley Hall (1958)

Helen Hadley Hall was named in memory of Mrs. Arthur Twining Hadley, wife of the thirteenth President of Yale. It is a residence hall for 205 women graduate students. The Hall has a number of "Fellows," who meet regularly and serve as advisers to the students.

Yale University Press (1959/60)

The Yale Press, founded in 1908, publishes between 75 and 80 original books, primarily for the academic community, and 20 paperbound reprints each year. While the Press is a department of the University, it serves scholars throughout the world. Its present home, remodeled from a bakery, contains editorial and publishing offices and the Carl Purington Rollins Printing-Office, which is responsible for all University printing and much of the printing of Press books.

Observatory (1956)
Bethany Observing Station (1958)

The present Observatory on the campus, formerly used by the Yerkes Laboratories of Primate Biology and then the Prospect Hill School, contains classrooms and workrooms as well as the Reed Telescope. Most observing, however, takes place nine miles away in Bethany, where a new 40-inch telescope has recently been added to the already installed Loomis Butler and Catalogue Camera telescopes.

281. Yale University Press, publishers and printers

282. Bethany Observing Station

283. Aerial view of the Yale–New Haven Medical Center and New Haven redevelopment area

The Medical Center

The Yale–New Haven Medical
Center, in the area bounded by
Howard, Congress, and Oak,
has been greatly expanded in the past
decade. The Memorial Unit, largely
devoted to the care of private patients,
was the product of an impressive
community financial drive which
followed the amalgamation resulting
in the Grace–New Haven Hospital
in 1951. In 1955, the Commonwealth Fund provided funds for the
Edward S. Harkness Memorial Hall,
which provides residential facilities
for married and unmarried medical
students. In the Hunter Radiation
Therapy Center (1957–58) the
attack on cancer continues; this was
one of the first Yale buildings to
which agencies of the U.S. Government made grants. The radiology
department uses the basement and
first floor, and the departments of
pediatrics and medicine occupy the
upper stories. Added to the older
Tompkins and Fitkin Pavilions, the
Dana Clinic (1964) contains the
hospital's central administrative areas,
as well as diagnostic facilities.

Laboratory of Clinical Investigation (1964/65)

The Laboratory of Clinical Investigation, a ten-story addition to the
School of Medicine, is the most recent
of the School's buildings. Here the
department of pediatrics studies
child development, biochemical
genetics, and pediatric cardiology,
and the department of medicine
carries on research into a wide variety
of diseases.

284. Laboratory of Clinical Investigation

a new world for men.

285. Laboratory of Epidemiology and Public Health

Laboratory of Epidemiology and Public Health (1963/64)

The gift of both private foundations and government, this laboratory on New Haven redevelopment land is the result of an important new relationship which in 1965 brought together the newly merged department of epidemiology and public health and the Rockefeller Foundation Virus Laboratories.

William B. Greeley Memorial Laboratory (1959)

This building of the School of Forestry, the oldest forestry school in the country, contains laboratories and facilities for the study of wood technology, forest genetics, tree physiology, and forest pathology. It was the first Yale structure to be designed by Paul Rudolph and is intended to symbolize the study of the forest, its Y-shaped columns spreading like trees to form a grove. The building stands just below Marsh Hall, the original home of the Forestry School.

Dunham Laboratory Wing (1958)

The first element in the plan to increase Yale's applied science facilities was the concrete and glass addition to the Dunham Laboratory for electrical engineering, built on the site of the Sheffield Mansion. The original laboratory was renovated at the same time to produce a completely integrated facility.

286. William B. Greeley Memorial Laboratory, School of Forestry

287. The new Dunham Laboratory

New methods aid progress everywhere,

288. The Yale Computer Center

Yale Computer Center (1961)

The Computer Center is equipped with the latest high-speed electronic computers, many of them the gift of the National Science Foundation, and contains a conference room, library, and lounge. Virtually every academic department uses the already overworked Center, and administrative data systems have also been instituted elsewhere in the University to handle financial, accounting, and general administrative routine.

Oceanography and Ornithology Laboratories (1959)

The new wing for the Bingham Oceanographic Laboratory combined with an Ornithological Laboratory was added to the west side of the Peabody Museum in 1959. The first two floors are used mainly for work in marine biology. They contain temperature-controlled aquarium rooms with fresh- and salt-water circulating systems, cold-storage space for specimens, a dark room, laboratories for graduate students and visiting scholars, and a library. In the third-floor ornithology laboratory, a large area set aside for specimens has an air-filtration system which eliminates impurities and controls the temperature. The basement is reserved for the Museum's work in anthropology and invertebrate zoology.

289. Classifying birds on the third floor, division of ornithology

290. Oceanography and Ornithology Laboratories, a wing of the Peabody Museum

291. Josiah Willard Gibbs Research Laboratories, Wright Nuclear Structure Laboratory in foreground

Josiah Willard Gibbs Research Laboratories (1955)

These laboratories were the first new facility for the sciences since 1922 and the forerunners of extensive construction on the Pierson-Sage Square. They were named for Josiah Willard Gibbs, one of America's greatest scientists and professor of mathematical physics at Yale from 1871 to 1903. Little known in his day, he was so dedicated to his work that he served on the faculty for ten years without pay, living on a small family income and private fees from students. He carried on pioneer work in thermodynamics with only pencil and paper, or on occasion blackboard and chalk as his tools. This building of glass, steel, and marble is used for advanced work in physical sciences. One of its special features is the "modular" unit, with a new type of panel wall which can easily be removed or placed to allow for changing research projects.

Arthur W. Wright Nuclear Structure Laboratory (1964)

The Nuclear Structure Laboratory was designed in a style called "Mayan Indian" to house the 20 mev tandem Van de Graff ("Emperor") accelerator. The "Emperor," the most accurate accelerator and the largest in the world, is the only one of its kind in this hemisphere. It is one of three at Yale, the others being the Heavy-Ion Accelerator and the Electron Accelerator, which were constructed between 1953 and 1961.

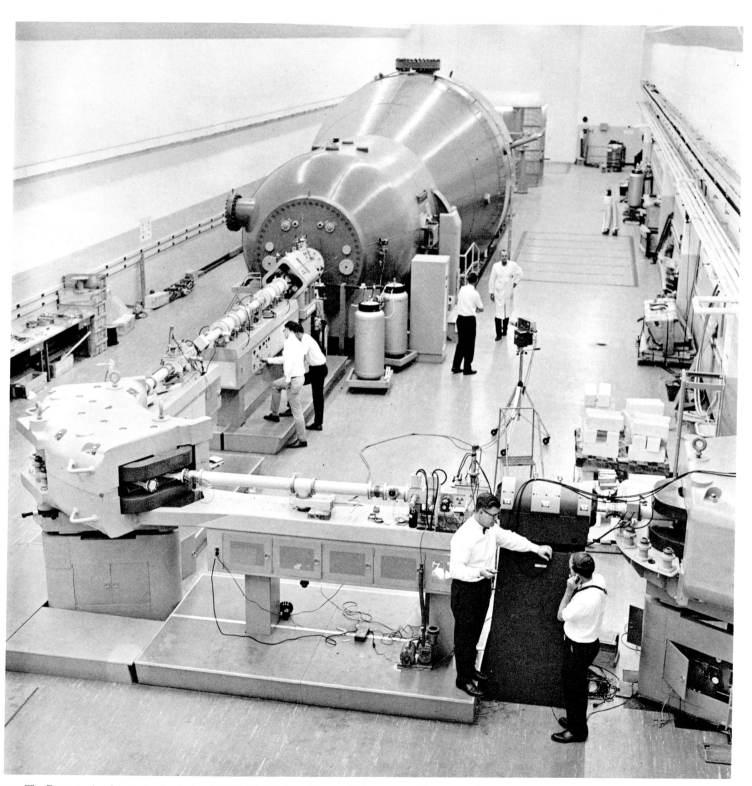

292. The Emperor Accelerator in the Arthur W. Wright Nuclear Structure Laboratory on Pierson-Sage Square

and towers above the past of Yale.

293. The Kline Geology Laboratory

294. The Kline Chemistry Laboratory

Kline Geology Laboratory (1962/63)

The Kline Geology Laboratory, the largest geologic center in the United States, like the other buildings in the Kline Science Center, was designed by Philip Johnson and named for the donor, C. Mahlon Kline, Ph.B. '01. All the laboratory walls in the building are movable. At the ground-breaking, President Griswold was confident in saying: "The turning of this earth marks a new era in Yale science, an era in which Yale at long last will have facilities for geology, biology, and chemistry, second to none in quality."

Kline Chemistry Laboratory (1963/64)

This research laboratory acommodates more than 150 graduate students, postdoctoral assistants, and faculty members. A U-shaped brick and sandstone building, it is connected to the northern end of Sterling Chemistry Laboratory.

Kline Biology Tower (1964/65)

The Kline Biology Tower, which unites the whole science complex, is a research center for the departments of biology and of molecular biophysics. The building, of reinforced concrete with brick and brownstone exterior, is fourteen stories high and is connected by tunnels to the Sloane Physics Laboratory and the Josiah Willard Gibbs Research Laboratories. It houses the University's Science Library at the lower level and a restaurant on the top floor.

295. The Kline Biology Tower rises above the campus

296. A tower view of the Yale campus and environs, 1966

The first date indicates year of construction or acquisition by Yale; second date is year of razing or sale by the University. Architect and donor are listed after name of each building where they are known. An asterisk indicates buildings not at present owned by Yale or the Yale–New Haven Hospital.

1717/18–1782	"Yale College." Henry Caner. Colony funds.
1722–1801	House for Rector (President). Henry Caner. Elihu Yale, church and private gifts, grant from General Assembly. Sold.
1750/53–	Connecticut Hall (South Middle College); *National Historic and New Haven Preservation Trust Landmark.* Francis Letort and Thomas Bills. General Assembly. 1797 alterations – Col. John Trumbull. College funds. 1905 – restoration – Grosvenor Atterbury; alumni gifts. 1952–54 restoration – Office of Douglas Orr and Richard A. Kimball; Old Dominion Foundation.
1757/58–?	House for Professor of Divinity. Unknown. President Clap and others.
1761/63–1893	First Chapel; Athenaeum 1824–93. Francis Letort and Thomas Bills. College funds.
1782–1888	Dining Hall and Kitchen; Old Laboratory 1820–88. Unknown. College funds.
1793/94–1893	Union Hall (South College). Unknown. Legislative grant.
1799–1860	Second Presidents' House; Analytical Laboratory, 1847–60. Peter Banner. Legislative grant and College funds.
1801–1895	Berkeley Hall (North Middle College). Peter Banner. Legislative grant.
1803/04–1901	Connecticut Lyceum. Peter Banner. Legislative grant.
1814–1931	Medical Institution; (South) Sheffield Hall, 1860–1931. Unknown. Purchased from James Hillhouse, College funds.
1819–1890	Commons; Philosophical Building (Cabinet), 1842–90. David Hoadley. College funds.
1820–1901	North College. Ira Atwater. College funds.
1823/24–1896	Second Chapel; classroom building, 1876–96. Unknown. Solicitation authorized by Corporation.
1832–1901	Trumbull Gallery; Treasury Building, 1868–1901. Col. John Trumbull. Legislative grant.
1833–1930	State Hospital (later North Ward), Y–NHH. Ithiel Town. Legislative grant and subscriptions.
1835–1869	Divinity College. Unknown. Sundry donors.
1842–	The College Library; Dwight Hall and Dwight Memorial Chapel, 1931. Henry Austin. Alumni subscriptions.
1851/53–1911	Alumni Hall (also called Graduates Hall). Alexander Jackson Davis. Linonia, Brothers in Unity, and Calliopean Literary Societies, and College funds.
*1856–	Skull and Bones.
1859–1917	Old Gymnasium; Dining Hall, 1892–1901; Herrick Hall, 1902–17. Chauncey A. Dickerman. College funds.
1859/60–1957	Medical School Building; leased to University of Connecticut College of Pharmacy, 1923; razed. Sidney Mason Stone. University funds. 1892 addition – Harrison W. Lindsley; College funds.

1860–1931	(South) Sheffield Hall ("Medical Institution," 1814–60). Purchased and enlarged, 1858. Unknown. Joseph E. Sheffield for Scientific School.
1864/66–	Art School Building; named Street Hall, 1928. Peter B. Wight. Augustus R. Street. 1963–64 interior modernization – Carleton Granbery and George Brower Cash; University funds.
1869/70–1931	East Divinity Hall; renamed Edwards Hall, 1909. Richard M. Hunt. Sundry donors.
1869/70–	Farnam Hall. Russell Sturgis, Jr. Henry Farnam.
*1869/70–	Scroll and Key. Richard M. Hunt.
1870/71–	Durfee Hall. Russell Sturgis, Jr. Bradford M. C. Durfee.
1871–1931	Marquand Chapel. Richard M. Hunt. Frederick Marquand.
1872/73–	North Sheffield Hall. J. Cleveland Cady. Joseph E. Sheffield.
1873–	East Ward, Y–NHH; renamed Tompkins East. Frederick C. Withers. Subscriptions.
1873–1931	West Ward, Y–NHH. Frederick C. Withers. Subscriptions.
1873/74–1931	West Divinity Hall; renamed Taylor Hall 1909. Rufus G. Russell. Sundry donors.
1873/76–1917	Peabody Museum. J. Cleveland Cady. George Peabody.
1874/76–	Battell Chapel. Russell Sturgis, Jr. Joseph Battell, his family, and other donors. 1893 addition – Cady, Berg & See; Robbins Battell. 1927 renovation – Everett V. Meeks; Mrs. Ellen (Battell) Stoeckel. 1947 apse remodeling – Richard M. Bennett and Andrew F. Euston; subscriptions.
1875–1910	Yale Boat House. Cummings & Sears. Sundry donors.
1876–1929	Power House and Laundry, Y–NHH. Unknown. Legislative grant and subscriptions.
1877–	56 Hillhouse Avenue; transferred to President Dwight in exchange for College Street residence, 1899; reacquired, 1928. Unknown. Mr. and Mrs. Frederic W. Stevens.
1881–1931	Trowbridge Library. E. E. Raht. Frederick Marquand.
1881–1931	Nurses' Dormitory, Y–NHH.
1882/83–1931	Sloane Physical Laboratory; renamed Sloane Lecture Hall, 1912. E. E. Raht. Henry T. Sloane and Thomas C. Sloane.
1882–	459 Prospect Street.
1882–1964	477 Prospect Street. Sold to the Day Prospect Hill School, 1964.
1882/83–1956	Observatory. Sold to the Day Prospect Hill School 1956. Rufus G. Russell. Oliver F. Winchester.
1885/86–	Lawrance Hall. Russell Sturgis, Jr. Mrs. Francis C. Lawrance.
1885/86–1926	Dwight Hall. J. Cleveland Cady. Elbert B. Monroe.
1886–1923	Superintendent's Quarters, Y–NHH. Unknown. Hospital funds.
1887/88–1931	Kent Chemical Laboratory; renamed Kent Hall 1922. E. E. Raht. Albert E. Kent and William Kent.
1888–1928	George Bronson Farnam Operating Amphitheatre, Y–NHH. Unknown. Mrs. Henry Farnam.
1888/90–1926	Osborn Hall. Bruce Price. Mrs. Miriam A. Osborn.

1888/90– Chittenden Library; renamed Linsly-Chittenden Hall, 1930. J. Cleveland Cady. Simeon B. Chittenden.

1889–1929 Gifford Ward – Ellen M. Gifford's Home for Incurables, Y–NHH. L. W. Robinson. Mrs. Ellen Marett Gifford.

1889–1957 Sheffield Biological Laboratory; Sheffield Laboratory of Physiological Chemistry, 1913–24; Laboratory of Applied Physiology, 1924–46; annex to Dunham Laboratory, 1946–57. Ithiel Town and A. J. Davis. 1859 enlargement – Henry Austin; Bequest of Joseph E. Sheffield.

1890/92–1932 University Gymnasium. E. E. Gandolfo. Sundry donors.

1891/92– Welch Hall. Bruce Price. Pierce N. Welch.

*1892–1929 Gifford Chapel, Y–NHH. L. W. Robinson. Mrs. Ellen Marett Gifford.

1892–1900 Psychological Laboratory. Unknown. Purchased.

1892– Yale Infirmary. J. C. Cady & Company. Many donors. 1906 addition – J. C. Cady & Company; Mrs. Charles P. Taft.

1892– Winchester Hall. J. C. Cady & Company. Mrs. Oliver F. Winchester.

1893–1917 Boiler House and Steam Department. Unknown. University funds.

1893/94–1933 Berkeley Hall. J. C. Cady & Company. University funds.

1893/94–1933 White Hall. Cady, Berg & See. Andrew J. White.

1894– Vanderbilt Hall. Charles C. Haight. Mr. and Mrs. Cornelius Vanderbilt.

1894/95– Sheffield Chemical Laboratory; renamed Sheffield Laboratory [of Engineering Mechanics] 1922. Cady, Berg & See. Funds of S.S.S. Trustees.

1894/1900– Hendrie Hall. Cady, Berg & See. John W. Hendrie and others.

1895–1917 College Street Hall. Purchased; sold 1917. Sidney Mason Stone. University funds.

1895–1932 125 High Street; named Gibbs Hall, 1916. Purchased. University funds.

1895– Whitman Memorial Gateway. Charles C. Haight. Mrs. Henry Farnam.

1896– Phelps Hall and Archway. Charles C. Haight. William Walter Phelps family. 1965–66 renovation – Granbery, Cash & Associates; University funds.

1896–1917 Pierson Hall. Cady, Berg & See. University funds.

1899–1930 Kitchen, Y–NHH. Attributed to L. W. Robinson. Hospital funds.

1899–1916 Music School Building. Unknown. University funds.

1899– Miller Memorial Gateway. Charles C. Haight. Class of 1897.

1899– Marsh Hall; built 1878; *National Historic Landmark.* J. C. Cady & Company. Bequest of Professor Othniel C. Marsh.

1900–1933 Round House, Berkeley Oval.

1900–1959 Maternity (South) Ward, Y–NHH. Attributed to L. W. Robinson. Hospital funds.

1900–1929 Medical Clinic Amphitheatre, Y–NHH. University funds.

1900/01–1933 Fayerweather Hall. Cady, Berg & See. Daniel B. Fayerweather.

1901– Jane Ellen Hope Memorial Building. L. W. Robinson. Mrs. Thomas G. Bennett.

*1901– Graduate Club Association; built 1799; *New Haven Preservation Trust Landmark.* David Hoadley. Purchased. 1902 addition – R. Clipston Sturgis.

*1901– Book and Snake. Louis R. Metcalfe.

1901– The Ninety-Six Memorial Gateway. H. Davis Ives. Class of 1896.

1901–   Woodbridge Hall. Howells & Stokes. The Misses Olivia Egleston Phelps
             Stokes and Caroline Phelps Stokes.

1901/02–   Bicentennial Buildings. Carrère & Hastings. Funds from alumni.

1902   Yale Field property given to the University.

1901–1917   Carpentry Department, 80 High Street. University funds.

1902/03–   Byers Hall (now part of Silliman College). Hiss & Weekes. Mrs. Alexander
             MacBurney Byers.

1902/03–   Kirtland Hall. Kirtland K. Cutter. Mrs. Lucy Hall Boardman. 1964–65
             interior modernization – Granbery, Cash & Associates; University funds.

1903/06–   Vanderbilt-Scientific Halls (Wall Street section now part of Silliman College;
             College Street building used by Law School). Charles C. Haight.
             Frederick W. Vanderbilt.

1903–1933   Lampson Lyceum and Hall. Cady, Berg & See. William Lampson.

1903/04–   Hammond [Metallurgical] Laboratory. W. Gedney Beatty. John Hays
             Hammond.

1905–   Gales Ferry Boat House. Unknown. Purchase and gifts.

1906/07–   Linsly Hall; named Linsly-Chittenden Hall, 1930. Charles C. Haight.
             William B. Ross.

1908–   Leet Oliver Memorial Hall. Charles C. Haight. Mrs. James Brown Oliver.

1909–1932   Carnegie Swimming Pool. Howells & Stokes. Andrew Carnegie.

1909–1933   Haughton Hall. R. H. Robertson & Son. William L. McLane.

*1909/10–1958 Adee Boat House. Sold 1958. Peabody & Stearns. Alumni.

1910   Pierson-Sage Square. Mrs. Russell Sage.

*1910–   Berzelius. Donn Barber.

1910/11–   Mason Laboratory [of Mechanical Engineering]. Charles C. Haight.
             William S. and George Grant Mason. 1966 alteration and renovation –
             Office of Douglas Orr, de Cossy, Winder & Associates; University funds.

1911–1931   Day Missions Library. Delano & Aldrich. The Reverend and Mrs. George
             Edward Day.

1911–   Elizabethan Club; built c. 1810–1815. Purchased. Gift of Alexander S. Cochran.

*1911/12–   Elihu; built c. 1772. Purchased. Additions and alterations – Everett V. Meeks.

1911/12–   Wright Memorial Hall. William Adams Delano. Alumni.

1911/12–   Sloane Physics Laboratory. Charles C. Haight. Henry T. and William D. Sloane.

1912–1929   Baseball Cage. L. W. Robinson. Alumni and friends.

1912–   Saint Elmo; see 1962 Yale Foreign Language Laboratory.

1912–   Daniels Memorial Gateway. Charles C. Haight. Mr. and Mrs. John W. Daniels.

1912–   Noah Porter Memorial Gateway. Howells & Stokes. Many friends.

*1912–   Mory's, 306 York Street. Purchased. Addition – Office of Douglas Orr.

1912/13–   Dunham Laboratory [of Electrical Engineering]. Henry G. Morse. Austin C.
             Dunham. 1958 addition – Office of Douglas Orr; Alumni. 1966 alteration
             and renovation – Office of Douglas Orr, de Cossy, Winder & Associates;
             University funds.

1913–   Pierson-Sage Boiler and Refrigeration Plant (formerly Pierson-Sage Heating Plant). Charles C. Haight. University funds. 1963–64 addition – Philip Johnson Associates; C. Mahlon Kline and University funds.

1913–   Land acquired for Yale Engineering Camp, East Lyme; *see* 1926.

1913–1930   Hopkins Hall. Purchased from Hopkins Grammar School.

*1913–   Saint Anthony Hall. Charles C. Haight.

1913/14–   Osborn Memorial Laboratories. Charles C. Haight. Bequest of Mrs. Miriam A. Osborn.

1913/14–   Yale Bowl. Charles A. Ferry. Gifts through Yale Committee of Twenty-One, Inc.

1914–1963   Isolation Pavilion (Howard Building), Y–NHH. L. W. Robinson. Sundry donors and City of New Haven.

1915–1957   Heliostat Building. Frank Miles Day and L. W. Robinson. University funds.

1915–1929   Squash Courts and Bowling Alleys. University funds.

1916/17–   Albert Arnold Sprague Memorial Hall. Coolidge & Shattuck. Mrs. Sprague and daughter, Mrs. Frederick S. Coolidge. *See* 1955, John Herrick Jackson Music Library.

1917/21–   Memorial Quadrangle; became Branford College and Saybrook College, 1933. James Gamble Rogers. Mrs. Stephen V. Harkness.

1917–   Yale Armory. Lansing, Bley & Lyman. A. Conger Goodyear.

1917–1927   Artillery Hall. University funds.

1917–   Boardman Administration Building, Y–NHH. Henry C. Pelton. Mrs. Lucy Hall Boardman.

1917–   Anthony N. Brady Memorial Laboratory. L. W. Robinson and Day & Klauder. Nicholas F. and James C. Brady. 1927 extension – Henry C. Pelton; General Education Board. 1964 fourth-floor rebuilding and basement renovation – Davis, Cochran & Miller; National Institutes of Health. 1965–66 second-floor alterations – Office of Douglas Orr, de Cossy, Winder & Associates; National Institutes of Health, Lions Eye Research Foundation.

1917/18–   University Heating and Power Plant and University Service Bureaus Building. Day & Klauder. Mrs. Stephen V. Harkness. 1927 addition – Charles Z. Klauder. 1954 storage and loading facilities – Leo F. Caproni. 1965 addition – Office of Douglas Orr, de Cossy, Winder & Associates; University funds.

1918–1927   Brady Laboratory Annex. Unknown. University funds.

1918–1957   Nathan Smith Hall. Purchased. Sold 1956; razed 1957.

1918–1948   William Wirt Winchester Hospital, Y–NHH. Sold. L. W. Robinson. Mrs. Sarah L. Winchester.

1918–   143 Elm Street; built 1831. *New Haven Preservation Trust Landmark.* Nahum Hayward. Gift of Mrs. James Harvey Williams for the Yale University Press.

1919–   66 Wall Street; built 1806 with entrance at 326 Temple Street. Purchased. 1922 remodeling – J. Frederick Kelly.

1919–   31 Hillhouse Avenue; built 1826. Unknown. Miss Martha Day Porter.

1920– 28 Hillhouse Avenue; built 1884; named Henry Barnard Hall, 1925. Purchased. Attributed to Russell Sturgis, Jr.

1921– Faculty Club; built 1764–67. *New Haven Preservation Trust Landmark.* Purchased. 1929 restoration – J. Frederick Kelly; a friend of the faculty. 1950–51 addition – Robert T. Coolidge; Mrs. James Rowland Angell and University funds. Kitchen addition – Henry Schwaub Kelly; sundry donors.

1921– 37 Hillhouse Avenue; built 1866. Purchased.

1921–1929 Health Department Building. Purchased.

1921– Alumni House 1958; built before 1812. Purchased.

1922–1929 Medical and Pediatric Laboratory. Unknown. General Education Board.

1922– Bowen Forest. Mrs. Edward S. Bowen.

1922– Winchester Building (formerly Private Pavilion), Y–NHH. Charles S. Palmer. Bond issue.

1922–1936 34 Hillhouse Avenue. Purchased.

1922/23– Sterling Chemistry Laboratory. Delano & Aldrich. John W. Sterling Estate.

1923/24– Sage Hall. William Adams Delano. William H. Sage.

1923– 52 Hillhouse Avenue; built 1849. *New Haven Preservation Trust Landmark.* Henry Austin. Purchased.

1923–1944 23 Hillhouse Avenue; built 1855. Purchased.

1923–1941 47 Hillhouse Avenue; built 1862. Purchased.

1923/24– Sterling Hall of Medicine. Charles Z. Klauder. John W. Sterling Estate. 1929–30 façade alterations – Grosvenor Atterbury. 1931 B Wing addition – Henry C. Pelton. 1957–58 C Wing addition – Office of Douglas Orr, de Cossy, Winder & Associates; Longwood Fund, United States Public Health Service, and University funds. 1965–66 B Wing Pharmacology alterations – same; Wellcome Trust of London. 1966–67 B Wing addition (animal facilities), same; United States Public Health Service, National Institutes of Health, University funds.

1923/24– Sterling Power House. Day & Klauder. John W. Sterling Estate. 1950 addition – David M. Hummel.

1923/24– Peabody Museum of Natural History. Charles Z. Klauder. Peabody Trustees and University funds. 1965 addition – Office of Douglas Orr, de Cossy, Winder & Associates; The Beinecke Foundation.

1924– 77 Prospect Street; built 1884. Purchased. McKim, Mead & White.

1924– 89 Trumbull Street. Purchased.

1924– 51 Hillhouse Avenue; built 1862. Purchased.

1924– Weir Hall. Plans by Tracy & Swartwout for George Douglas Miller. Purchased unfinished, 1917. Completed by Everett V. Meeks. 1932 addition – James Gamble Rogers; Edward S. Harkness and University funds. 1965, western section converted into Robert A. Taft Library, Jonathan Edwards College.

1924– Bob Cook Boat House. James Gamble Rogers. Alumni.

1924– Lapham Field House. Day & Klauder. Henry G. Lapham.

*1924/26– Wolf's Head. Bertram G. Goodhue.

1925–1963	Southern Hemisphere Telescope, at University of the Witwatersrand, Johannesburg, 1925–52, Commonwealth Observatory, Mount Stromlo, Canberra, Australia, 1952. Roland W. Sellew. University funds.
1925–	Edwin McClellan Hall. Walter B. Chambers. Mrs. McClellan.
1925–	301 Prospect Street. Purchased.
1926–	87 Trumbull Street. Purchased.
1926–	Yale Golf Course. Charles B. McDonald. Mrs. Sarah Wey Tompkins.
1925/26–	Dickinson and Wheelock halls; incorporated into Jonathan Edwards College, 1932. James Gamble Rogers. Robert M. Judson.
1925/26–	University Theatre. Blackall, Clapp & Whittemore. 1957 addition – Henry F. Miller; Edward S. Harkness.
1926–	Phipps Polo Field. John S., Henry C., and Howard Phipps, and the Honorable Mrs. Frederick E. Guest.
1926–	Tracy Hall and other buildings, Yale Engineering Camp, East Lyme. Office of Douglas Orr. Yale Engineering Association.
1926/27–	William L. Harkness Hall. William Adams Delano. Mr. Harkness and family.
1926/28–	Charles W. Bingham Hall. Walter B. Chambers. Sons and daughters of Mr. Bingham.
1927–	Baseball stands, Yale Field. University funds.
1927–	Charles E. Coxe Memorial Gymnasium. Lockwood, Greene & Company. C. E. Coxe Family.
1927–	340 Edwards Street Laboratory. Unknown. Bequest of Mrs. Henry C. White.
1927–	Alumni War Memorial. Thomas Hastings and Everett V. Meeks. Alumni.
1927/28–	Lauder Hall. Henry C. Pelton. General Education Board. 1961 fourth-floor addition – Warren & Wetmore; Charles A. Dana, John Day Jackson family, Victoria Foundation, National Institutes of Health.
1927/28–	Farnam Memorial Building. Henry C. Pelton. General Education Board.
1927/28–	(Old) Art Gallery. Egerton Swartwout. Edward S. Harkness.
1927/28–	Walter Camp Field. John W. Cross. Contributions from 503 schools and colleges and Yale alumni.
1927/30–	Sterling Memorial Library. James Gamble Rogers. John W. Sterling Estate. 1964–65 alterations – J. Russell Bailey; University funds.
*1928	Berkeley Divinity School moved to New Haven.
1928–	DeWitt Cuyler Field at Yale Field.
1928–1954	88 Trumbull Street. Purchased. Sold.
1928–	Sterling Dormitory. Purchased. Roy W. Foote. John W. Sterling Estate. Sold to Hospital, 1957.
*1928–	Fence Club. James Gamble Rogers.
*1929–	Zeta Psi. Everett V. Meeks.
1929/30–	Raleigh Fitkin Memorial Pavilion. Henry C. Pelton. Abram E. Fitkin. Title transferred to Hospital, 1952.
1929/30–	Laboratory for Medicine and Pediatrics. Henry C. Pelton. General Education Board.

1929/30– Institute of Human Relations. Grosvenor Atterbury. Rockefeller Foundation and General Education Board.

1929/30– Department of University Health Building. Cross & Cross. University funds.

1929/33– Trumbull College. James Gamble Rogers. John W. Sterling Estate.

1929/31– Clinic Building, Y–NHH. Henry C. Pelton. General Education Board. 1962 installation, Diagnostic Radiology Section – John A. Hartford Foundation, Inc., Fannie E. Rippel Foundation, New Haven Foundation, and United States Government (Hill-Burton Act), and sundry donors.

1930– 15 Hillhouse Avenue; built 1894–95 for Alpha Delta Phi. Unknown. Purchased. Now occupied by Collection of Musical Instruments.

1930/31– Sterling Law Buildings. James Gamble Rogers. John W. Sterling Estate. 1966 underground extension Law Library – Skidmore, Owings & Merrill; United States Department of Health, Education, and Welfare, Law School Capital Funds Program.

1930/31– Pierson College. James Gamble Rogers. Edward S. Harkness.

*1930– Delta Kappa Epsilon. James Gamble Rogers.

1930– Linsly-Chittenden Hall; *see* 1888–90, 1906–07.

1930–1960 325–327 Temple Street. L. W. Robinson. Purchased; sold.

1930/32– Hall of Graduate Studies. James Gamble Rogers. John W. Sterling Estate.

1930/32– Payne Whitney Gymnasium. John Russell Pope. Mrs. Whitney and children, Mrs. Charles S. Payson and John Hay Whitney.

1930/32– Davenport College. James Gamble Rogers. Edward S. Harkness.

1931– William Whitman Farnam Memorial Garden. Gift of his widow.

1931– 202 Prospect Street. Purchased.

1931– Bowers Hall. Delano & Aldrich. Edward A. Bowers.

1931– 55 Hillhouse Avenue; built 1859. *New Haven Preservation Trust Landmark.* Sidney Mason Stone. Purchased.

1931– Dwight Hall and Dwight Memorial Chapel. Charles Z. Klauder. University funds. *See* 1842–46 College Library.

1931/32– Sterling Divinity Quadrangle. Delano & Aldrich. John W. Sterling Estate. 1954 Divinity School Library remodeling – J. Russell Bailey and Andrew F. Euston; University funds.

1931/32– Sheffield Hall, Sterling Tower, Strathcona Hall. Zantzinger, Borie & Medary. S.S.S. Trustees, John W. Sterling Estate, and bequest of Lord Strathcona and Mount Royal.

1931/32– Ray Tompkins House. John Russell Pope. Mrs. Sarah Wey Tompkins.

1931/32– Calhoun College. John Russell Pope. Edward S. Harkness.

1931/32– Briton Hadden Memorial Building. Adams & Prentice. Alumni and friends of Yale.

1932– 204 Prospect Street. Purchased.

*1932– John B. Pierce Foundation Laboratory. H. Lansing Quick.

1932– Jonathan Edwards College. James Gamble Rogers. Edward S. Harkness. 1965 The Robert A. Taft Library, converted from part of Weir Hall –

Charles H. Brewer, Jr.; William Howard Taft, 3d, and other Fellows, alumni, and associates of the College.

1931/33–   Sarah Wey Tompkins Memorial Pavilion. Henry C. Pelton. Mrs. Tompkins. Title transferred to Hospital, 1952.

1933–   Branford College and Saybrook College. James Gamble Rogers. Edward S. Harkness. Converted from Memorial Quadrangle.

1933–   Mouse House, School of Medicine. David M. Hummel. The Jane Coffin Childs Memorial Fund for Medical Research.

1933–   1 Hillhouse Avenue (formerly 131 Grove Street); built 1888 as The Cloister (Book and Snake). 1917 addition – Clarence H. Stilson; Stone Trust Association.

1933–   17 Hillhouse Avenue; built 1898 as The Colony for Berzelius Trust Association. Brite & Bacon. Purchased.

1933/34–   Timothy Dwight College. James Gamble Rogers. Edward S. Harkness.

1933/34–   Berkeley College. James Gamble Rogers. Edward S. Harkness.

1934/37–   The President's House; built 1871. Russell Sturgis, Jr. Bequest of Henry Farnam.

*1934–1940   Sachem Hall (Phi Sigma Kappa); built 1907. Purchased. Sold to Berkeley Divinity School, 1940.

1934–   370 Temple Street; built 1906 as Vernon Hall (Phi Gamma Delta). Satterlee & Boyd. Purchased.

1935–   27 Hillhouse Avenue; built 1866. Purchased.

1935–   Beta Theta Pi; built 1926–27. James Gamble Rogers. Purchased. Leased to fraternity.

1935–   96 Wall Street; named Stoeckel Hall 1956; built 1897 as York Hall (Chi Phi). Grosvenor Atterbury. Purchased.

1935–   451 College Street; built 1910–11 as Franklin Hall (Theta Xi). Chapman & Frazer. Purchased.

1935–   215 Park Street; built 1931. James Gamble Rogers. Gift of Alpha Delta Phi.

1937–   Drama Annex; built 1930 for Alpha Chi Rho. Delano & Aldrich. Purchased.

*1938–   St. Thomas More Chapel and More House. Office of Douglas Orr. 1959–60 addition – William Douglas; alumni of Roman Catholic faith.

1940–   Yale Forestry Camp. Sterling W. and Edward C. Childs.

1940–   Silliman College; includes Byers Hall 1902–03 and part of Vanderbilt-Scientific Halls 1903–06. Eggers & Higgins. Bequest of Frederick W. Vanderbilt.

1941–   Yale Medical Library. Grosvenor Atterbury. John W. Sterling Estate.

1943   Sachem's Wood; land acquired by bequest of Mrs. James Hillhouse.

1945–   University News Bureau Building; built 1928 for the *Yale Record*. Lorenzo Hamilton. Purchased.

1945–   493 College Street; built 1913 as part of Saint Anthony Hall. Charles C. Haight. Purchased.

1948–   38 Hillhouse Avenue. Bruce Price. Purchased. Sold to Berkeley Divinity School; reacquired by University for use as Office of Undergraduate Admissions and Freshman Scholarships, 1961. Renumbered 111 Prospect Street.

1948–   Laundry, Y–NHH. Office of Douglas Orr. Hospital funds, United States Public Health Service, and general subscription.

1950–	217 Park Street; built 1930–31. James Gamble Rogers. Gift of Phi Gamma Delta.
1951/53–	Memorial Unit, Y–NHH. Office of Douglas Orr. Subscriptions.
1952–	Grace–New Haven School of Nursing. Office of Douglas Orr. Hospital funds.
1952–	Animal Care Facility. Office of Douglas Orr. United States Public Health Service.
*1953–	Veterans Administration Hospital, West Haven. William A. Riley. United States Government.
1953–	New Art Gallery. Louis I. Kahn and Office of Douglas Orr. Hugh Campbell, alumni, and friends.
1953–	35 Hillhouse Avenue; built 1837. *New Haven Preservation Trust Landmark.* Alexander Jackson Davis. Purchased.
1953/55–	Accelerator Laboratories. Office of Douglas Orr. Atomic Energy Commission and alumni.
1953/55–	Edward S. Harkness Memorial Hall. Gugler, Kimball & Husted, and Office of Douglas Orr. The Commonwealth Fund.
1954–	Divinity School Library addition. J. Russell Bailey and Andrew F. Euston. University funds.
1954–	30 Hillhouse Avenue; built 1884, remodeled 1908. Purchased.
1955–	Josiah Willard Gibbs Research Laboratories. Paul Schweikher with Office of Douglas Orr. Alumni and friends. 1958 addition – same; John A. Hartford Foundation, Inc., and the United States Public Health Service.
1955–	John Herrick Jackson Music Library, Sprague Memorial Hall. J. Russell Bailey. The Jackson family.
1956–	295 Crown Street. Bequest of Mrs. Katherine B. Ingersoll.
1956–	Observatory, 135 Prospect Street. Purchased. Addition and remodeling – Andrew F. Euston.
1956/58–	York Square houses. Purchased.
1957–	The George P. Brett Pinetum, Fairfield, Conn. Gift.
1957–	297 Crown Street. Purchased.
1957–	Divinity School residences. Office of Douglas Orr. Sealantic Fund, Inc.
1957/58–	Hunter Radiation Therapy Center. Office of Douglas Orr. Robert E. Hunter, the United States Public Health Service, and the United States Government (Hill-Burton Act). 1965–66 additional three floors – Office of Douglas Orr, de Cossy, Winder & Associates; National Institutes of Health, The Lawrence M. Gelb Foundation, The John and Mary R. Markle Foundation, Mr. Hunter, The Bill Hahn Foundation, and the New Haven Foundation.
1957/58–	David S. Ingalls Rink. Eero Saarinen. The Ingalls family and friends of Yale hockey.
1958–	Maintenance Building, Y–NHH. Office of Douglas Orr. Ford Foundation.
1958–	Helen Hadley Hall. Office of Douglas Orr. The Rubicon Foundation, Inc., Eugene Meyer, Mrs. Pare Lorentz, and Malcolm P. Aldrich.
1958–	The Observing Station, Bethany. Andrew F. Euston. Mrs. James E. Cooper, James W. Cooper, and The Rubicon Foundation, Inc.

1958/59–	Bingham Oceanographic Laboratory. Office of Douglas Orr. William Robertson Coe, Wendell W. Anderson, Harry Payne Bingham, and others.
1959–	York–Crown Apartments. Purchased. Remodeled by Charles Brewer, Jr.
1959–	Clubhouse, Yale Golf Course. Andrew F. Euston. Alumni.
1959–	William B. Greeley Memorial Laboratory. Paul Rudolph. John A. Hartford Foundation, Inc., and subscriptions.
1959/60–	Yale University Press Building. Remodeled by Carleton Granbery. Purchased.
1960–	302 Temple Street; built 1843. Ithiel Town. 1885 addition – L. W. Robinson. 1912 alterations – R. W. Foote. Purchased.
1960–	211 Park Street, Offices, Yale Student Center and International Student Center of New Haven, Inc.; built 1929 for Chi Psi. H. Herbert Wheeler. Purchased.
1960–	254 Prospect Street. Purchased.
1960–	Animal Care Farm, Bethany, Conn. Davis, Cochran & Miller. 1964 addition – Office of Douglas Orr, de Cossy, Winder & Associates; National Institutes of Health, University funds.
1960/61–	Mary S. Harkness Memorial Auditorium. Office of Douglas Orr, de Cossy, Winder & Associates. The Commonwealth Fund.
1960/61–	Mansfield Street Apartments (291–311). Paul Rudolph. University funds.
1961–	218 Prospect Street. Purchased.
1961–	285 Prospect Street. Bequest of Ralph G. VanName.
1960/62–	Morse College. Eero Saarinen. Property, John Hay Whitney; buildings, Old Dominion Foundation.
1960/62–	Ezra Stiles College. Eero Saarinen. Property, John Hay Whitney; buildings, Old Dominion Foundation.
1961/62–	Yale Computer Center. Skidmore, Owings & Merrill. Arthur K. Watson and Mrs. Thomas J. Watson.
*1961/62–	Yale Co-Operative Corporation. Eero Saarinen. University funds.
1961/63–	Art and Architecture Building. Paul Rudolph. Alumni, friends, and the Helen and Thomas Hastings Fund, Inc.
1961/63–	The Beinecke Rare Book and Manuscript Library. Skidmore, Owings & Merrill. Edwin J., Frederick W., and Mrs. Walter Beinecke, and other members of family.
1962–	Southern Observatory, El Leoncito, Argentina. Carmen Renard. The Ford Foundation.
*1962–	Manuscript. King Lui Wu.
1962–	Dana House; built 1849. *National Historic and New Haven Preservation Trust Landmark.* Henry Austin. Purchased.
1962–	Yale Foreign Language Laboratory; built 1912 for St. Elmo (Rhinelander Trust Association). Kenneth M. Murchison. Purchased.
1962–	Esplanade Apartments. Purchased.
1962/63–	Kline Geology Laboratory. Philip Johnson Associates. C. Mahlon Kline, National Science Foundation.
1963/64–	Kline Chemistry Laboratory. Philip Johnson Associates. C. Mahlon Kline,

National Science Foundation, National Institutes of Health, United States Public Health Service.

1963/64– Laboratory of Epidemiology and Public Health. Philip Johnson Associates and Office of Douglas Orr. Rockefeller Foundation, National Institutes of Health, bequest of Baroness Elisabeth von Elverfeldt, Avalon Foundation, James Foundation, and University funds.

1963/64– Arthur W. Wright Nuclear Structure Laboratory. Office of Douglas Orr, de Cossy, Winder & Associates. Atomic Energy Commission and National Science Foundation.

1963/64– Charles A. Dana Clinic and Hospital Diagnostic and Service Building, Y–NHH. E. Todd Wheeler and The Perkins & Will Partnership. The Charles A. Dana Foundation, Inc., The Kresge Foundation, The Surdna Foundation, Inc., Women's Auxiliary of the Hospital, and friends.

1964– Whitehall Apartments. Purchased.

*1964/65– B'nai B'rith Hillel Foundation. Purchased. Renovation – Charles H. Abramowitz.

1964/65– Kline Biology Tower. Philip Johnson and Richard Foster. C. Mahlon Kline, National Institutes of Health, National Science Foundation.

1964/65– Laboratory of Clinical Investigation. Office of Douglas Orr, de Cossy, Winder & Associates, and E. Todd Wheeler and The Perkins & Will Partnership. National Institutes of Health, Commonwealth Fund, and Victoria Foundation, Inc.

*1964/66– Connecticut Mental Health Center. Pedersen & Tilney. State of Connecticut.

1966– Perinatal Research Center, Memorial Unit, Y–NHH. Office of Douglas Orr, de Cossy, Winder & Associates. Mrs. Charles A. Dana, United States Government (Hill-Burton Act), and others.

Bibliography

Lyman H. Bagg, *Four Years at Yale,* New Haven, 1891.

Walter Camp and L. S. Welch, *Yale: Her Campus, Classrooms and Athletics,* Boston, 1899.

Arnold G. Dana, "Yale Old and New," 78 vols. personal scrapbook, 1942.

Clarence Deming, *Yale Yesterdays,* New Haven, Yale University Press, 1915.

Franklin B. Dexter, *Biographical Sketches of Graduates of Yale: Yale College with Annals of the College History,* 6 vols. New York, 1885–1912.

Robert Dudley French, *The Memorial Quadrangle,* New Haven, Yale University Press, 1929.

Edgar S. Furniss, *The Graduate School of Yale,* New Haven, 1965.

William L. Kingsley, *Yale College: A Sketch of its History,* 2 vols. New York, 1879.

Edwin Oviatt, *The Beginnings of Yale (1701–1726),* New Haven, Yale University Press, 1916.

George Wilson Pierson, *Yale College, An Educational History (1871–1921),* New Haven, Yale University Press, 1952.
Yale, The University College (1921–1937), New Haven, Yale University Press, 1955.

Anson Phelps Stokes, *Memorials of Eminent Yale Men,* 2 vols. New Haven, Yale University Press, 1914.

Yale Alumni Weekly, 1–46 (1890–1937).

Yale Alumni Magazine, 1–29 (1937–66).

Yale Daily News, 1–87 (1878–1966); "Fiftieth Anniversary Issue," 1928; "Seventy-Five," 1953.

Yale University, Office of the Secretary, *Yale's Graduate and Professional Schools,* 1954; *The Buildings of Yale University,* 1965; *The Residential Colleges at Yale University,* 1967.

Miscellaneous University pamphlets and bulletins.